Luther and the Jews

Luther and the Jews

Putting Right the Lies

Richard S. Harvey

CASCADE *Books* • Eugene, Oregon

LUTHER AND THE JEWS
Putting Right the Lies

Cascade Books
An Imprint of Wipf and Stock Publishers
199 W. 8th Ave., Suite 3
Eugene, OR 97401

www.wipfandstock.com

PAPERBACK ISBN: 978-1-5326-1901-4
HARDCOVER ISBN: 978-1-4982-4501-2
EBOOK ISBN: 978-1-4982-4500-5

Cataloguing-in-Publication data:

Names: Harvey, Richard.

Title: Luther and the Jews : putting right the lies / Richard S. Harvey.

Description: Eugene, OR: Cascade Books, 2017 | Includes bibliographi-
cal references.

Identifiers: ISBN 978-1-5326-1901-4 (paperback) | ISBN 978-1-4982-
4501-2 (hardcover) | ISBN 978-1-4982-4500-5 (ebook)

Subjects: LCSH: Luther, Martin, 1483–1546—Relation with Jews | Chris-
tianity and antisemitism | Antisemitism—Germany | Antisemistism |
Messianic Judaism

Classification: BR333.5.J4 H375 2017 (print) | BR333.5.J4 (ebook)

Manufactured in the U.S.A.   06/30/17

To Monica—"A woman of worth who can find?"
(Proverbs 31:10)

אֵשֶׁת־חַיִל מִי יִמְצָא וְרָחֹק מִפְּנִינִים מִכְרָהּ׃

Contents

·

Preface

I WAS WEEPING UNCONTROLLABLY. THE inhuman stillness of Buchenwald concentration camp in Eastern Germany had got to me. I was with a party of German and Austrian Christians, many of them children of former SS guards and members of the Nazi party, to pray, repent, and seek reconciliation and forgiveness from one another and from the Lord. We met at a conference center in Volkenroda run by the Bruderhof, the Brothers of Jesus, a group of Protestants committed to work and pray for the spiritual renewal and re-uniting of all the streams within the Body of Christ.

It had not been my intention to visit a concentration camp, but it was on the schedule to visit the camp to remember the life and ministry of Pastor Paul Schneider, who was incarcerated and died in one of the torture chambers at the entrance. His small cell where he spent his last days is now something of a shrine, and our group had gone to say prayers there, honor his memory, and leave some flowers.

But Jews don't do flowers at funerals! Our funerals are always sad, mournful affairs, at a graveside. We put a stone on the tombstone, as a way of adding to the memorial that has already been set up. So I walked the short distance from the camp entrance to the place where hut 49 stood, now dedicated to the memory of those eleven thousand Jewish people among the 56,545 who died in the camp. There I recited the *kaddish* prayer, a Hebrew prayer that Jesus himself would have been familiar with, and whose phrases re-occur in the Lord's Prayer, the prayer he taught his disciples. I recited the *kaddish*, remembering my family, some of whom died in the camps, and my people, and the sufferings of others who died there—homosexuals, travelers, the physically and mentally incapacitated—and I wept.

I do not normally break down in tears, but it is a gift that God has given me at various times over the years, and as I sat down outside the camp and wept, a lady took my arm, and walked with me. Patty B, a Thai Christian now living in Chicago, understood something of what I was feeling. A Catholic from a Buddhist/animist culture, she knew the pain of being separated from her people, culture, and identity. In common humanity she took my arm and walked with me into the camp entrance. She told me later: "I did not want you to be alone."

I do not like to trivialize experiences, far less write about them for commercial purposes, but I knew that this experience would profoundly shape my thoughts and feelings for some time to come. As I looked on the place of slaughter of so many of my people, I knew I would have to process, think, and reflect on this terrible experience of sorrow and sadness, and pray. Earlier in the conference I had spoken about repentance and reconciliation in the Body of Christ in the light of the first split in the church, that between Jewish and non-Jewish believers in Jesus. Here I was at a conference of Protestant and Catholic Christians, speaking as a Messianic Jew—a Jewish believer in Yeshua (Jesus)—on the need for true reconciliation in his love. But in the midst of their concerns, for unity within the Body of Christ, here was I, a Jewish believer in Jesus, having to come to terms, both emotionally, spiritually, and theologically, with the depth of pain and suffering inflicted on my people by those who had been caught up in the horror of Nazism. People who called themselves Christians, who lived in a Christian country, churchgoers who had their children baptized and confirmed, were married in church, and tried to live according to Christian principles. Yet they had done so little to stop the rounding up, deportation, and murder of six million Jewish people.

So where to begin? We were there to meet for prayer, repentance, and confession in the run up to Wittenberg 2017, the 500th anniversary of Martin Luther's nailing of ninety-five theses on the door of the Castle Church in Wittenberg, a small town over one hundred miles away. This event effectively launched the Protestant Reformation, which would change the face of Europe and the nature of the church for centuries. The cornerstone of Luther's theology, that we are saved by grace through faith, and not by our own good deeds or works of righteousness, is something with which I heartily concurred. But the additional baggage of Luther's teachings, his many writings and sermons against the Jews, had done irreparable damage to Jewish-Christian relations. His writings, reprinted by the Nazis and used by Hitler for his propaganda campaign to argue for the Final Solution to the Jewish Question—to have them all destroyed—casts a terrible, dark shadow over Christianity in Europe, and inflicts a deep trauma and psychological wound that still affects Jewish people today.

Acknowledgments

THIS BOOK WAS BIRTHED in the meetings for repentance, prayer, and reconciliation between Protestants, Catholics, and Messianic Jews held by the Wittenberg 2017 "Way of Reconciliation" initiative (http://wittenberg2017.eu/). I am particularly grateful for the encouragement of Ludwig, Cecily, and Hubertus Benecke, Benjamin Berger, Amy and Thomas Cogdell, Peter Hocken, Hans-Peter and Verena Lang, George and Hanna Miley, the Psalm family, David and Greetje Sanders, Julia Stone, and Sisters Joela and Laetitia for their prayers, support, and encouragement. I am most grateful to my editor Robin Parry for his usual expertise and encouragement.

Dr. Richard Harvey is a Senior Researcher with Jews for Jesus and Associate Lecturer, All Nations Christian College. This book is his personal opinion and does not represent the views of any other individual or organization.

Can Anything Good Come Out of Wittenberg?

O CTOBER 2017 SEES THE 500th anniversary of Luther's nail-ing of his famous ninety-five theses to the door of the Castle Church in Wittenberg. Luther's action may have started the Reformation; he was certainly one of its architects.

Luther was a man of vision, and courage. He was however also profoundly anti-Semitic, and his sermons against the Jews were reprinted by Adolf Hitler in his campaign for a Final Solu-tion. Luther's legacy still casts a shadow across the world. With the 500th anniversary in prospect, it is time to examine what he said, the impact of his words, and to see what Catholics, Protestants, and Jews alike can do to heal the divisions that Luther fostered so terribly.

My friend Mark Kinzer and I were in Moscow for a meeting of the Helsinki Consultation on Jewish Continuity in the Body of Christ, an ecumenical gathering of Jewish believers in Jesus from many different denominational backgrounds, including Russian Orthodox, Roman Catholic, Baptist, Pentecostal, and Messianic Jewish congregations.

I was describing my book project to coincide with the 500th anniversary celebrations in 2017 of the birthing of Protestantism under Martin Luther, my fascination and arguments with his life, writings, and legacy, and my hope that the issues of Martin Luther and the Jews would be of interest both to Lutherans and Jews, particularly Jewish believers in Yeshua (Jesus).

Mark asked a question which struck to the very heart of the project: "What did Luther say that is of value for Messianic Jews that has not already been said better by others?" In other words, why bother with Luther, when the overall effect of his contribution has been bad news for Jews throughout history, and anything good that Luther did have to say was already available in the writings and teachings of others? I know that Mark has been more influenced by (Roman) Catholic theology and moved more in Catholic spheres, so his question was a fair one: why bother with Luther?

I had to think quickly for a few minutes. I know that what for Protestants is perhaps his greatest contribution, the restoration of the doctrine of justification by faith, has been seriously challenged and revised by those proposing the "New Perspective on Paul." They have argued that Luther was imposing on his battles with the pope and papal authority in the Church of Rome a somewhat inaccurate and misleading construction of the nature of rabbinic Judaism at the time of Christ, which appeared to him to demand justification by works of the law as the means of satisfying God's requirements for righteousness. For Catholics, such a misreading of their position—which was subsequently modified to correct such a misunderstanding during the Counter-Reformation in general, and the Council of Trent in particular—was not a blessing.

What I came up with was a restatement of the centrality of Christ, of grace, of Scripture, and of faith—Luther's solas—couched in a way that was not inimical either to Roman Catholics or to Jews, but it was hard work. I also spoke about Luther's sacramental theology, his practical and user-friendly teaching materials in his shorter and longer catechisms, his spirituality and depth of devotion. But it was challenging, and I do not think I convinced my friend. And this is why this book is necessary.

I want my Lutheran friends and those indebted to Martin Luther and his theology to have something good to say about him—good news for Jews and Jewish believers in Jesus especially—that will be well-received, understood, and appreciated. Likewise I want my Jewish family and friends, and especially Messianic Jews, to engage with the many positives that can be found in Martin Luther's life, learning, and legacy, and not dwell exclusively on the undeniably significant and overwhelming legacy of his anti-Judaism and anti-Semitism, which resulted in the worst disasters and harshest treatment the Jewish people received at the hands of so-called Christians, and the death of 6 million Jews during the Holocaust.

In the decade leading up to the celebration of Luther's 500th anniversary there have been many themes and emphases taken up by scholars, church leaders, public events, and activities. The 2017 Kirchentag event in Berlin will bring together some 200,000 German Christians with a focus on Wittenberg, Luther's home and base. Some attention has already been given to "Luther and the Jews," but in my opinion, not enough. The responses to his teaching and its effect have been rightly repentant, and judiciously thoughtful, but I would like to see us go further in exploring the roots and nature of his anti-Jewish polemic, and then constructively explore options for repentance, renewal, reconciliation, and restoration of relationships, particularly between German Christians and Jewish people. I also want to see Luther's theology, with its sharp contrasts between the old and new covenants, and between the church and the Jewish people, strongly challenged and revised.

Then I want to see the Jewish engagement with Luther renewed and revised. What do Jews who have become Lutherans have to say? How do they understand the problematic conception of the church membership in the light of their peoplehood? What value does their ethnic and religious identity as Jews still hold, in the light of their confession of faith in Yeshua and their membership of Lutheran churches?

As Christians from all denominations join with Lutherans in their celebration of the 500th anniversary of the start of Martin Luther's Reformation, for one group (at least) the celebrations are deeply problematic and bittersweet. These are Jewish believers in Jesus who cannot ignore the legacy of Luther's anti-Judaism and its tragic effects on their families and relationships with Lutherans today. These Messianic Jews believe that Jesus is the Messiah while retaining aspects of their Jewish ethnic, cultural, and religious identity.[1]

I write as a Jewish believer in Jesus, born in the United Kingdom, brought up in the Liberal Jewish Synagogue ("Reform" in the US), who became a believer in Jesus in the 1970s.[2]

My family originates from Germany, having changed their name from Hirschland to Harvey in the 1930s, so my interest in Jewish-Christian relations and the German-Jewish experience has been deeply personal. As a theologian within the Messianic movement I have a particular interest in reconciliation, both between Messianic Jews and Palestinian Christians in the light of the Israeli-Palestinian conflict, and also between Jews and Germans in the light of the Shoah.

In the pages that follow we will explore the questions "Who was Martin Luther?" and "What did he have to say about the Jewish people?" We will contrast this by asking "Who are the Jewish people?" and "What was the effect of Luther's teaching on the Jews and their religion?" With those four questions under our belt, we will then ask "What needs to happen today?" and "How can Christians, especially Lutherans and those celebrating the 500th anniversary of this colossal figure in the history of Christianity, put right the lies that Luther told about the Jewish people?"

This is not an easy story to tell. Most Jewish people know very little about Martin Luther, and what they do know is generally very bad: he was a persecutor of our people, and his lies led eventually to the genocidal attempt of Adolph Hitler and the Nazis to wipe the Jewish people off the face of the earth. Most Lutherans, on the other hand, inherit a great sense of guilt at the way Luther taught about and wanted the Jewish people to be treated, but have not found practical ways of putting right the lies. They have sometimes, even unwittingly, perpetuated them or allowed them to go unchallenged, both theologically and in day-to-day

1. Harvey, *Mapping Messianic Jewish Theology*, 7. For literature on the Messianic Movement see Chapter 8: Further Reading and Resources.

2. Harvey, *But I'm Jewish*, 8.

Jewish-Christian relations. I do not claim to have all the answers, or even some of them, but as a Jewish believer in Jesus whose family originates from Germany and who has an admiration for much of the good that Luther discovered and taught, I urgently want something to be done so that the lies may be put right, and my own people might hear from Lutherans not bad news, but good.

CHAPTER I

Who was Martin Luther?

Early Life

L ATE IN THE EVENING of 10 November 1483 the first of nine children was born to Hans and Margarethe Luder[1] of Eisleben in the county of Mansfeld, in the central region of Germany. The following day he was baptized in the Church of St. Peter and St. Paul, and given the name of the saint of that day, Martin (of Tours).

Hans and Margarethe were hard-working farming people, but Hans did not inherit the family farm in Möhra, and moved eighty miles away from friends and family to Eisleben, where he become a miner in the hope of earning a better living in the local copper mine. Hard work and tight control of the family finances made him a successful and well-to-do merchant. Margarethe also worked hard to bring up the large family, and Martin grew up knowing his parents also had high expectations of him. A university education, a successful career in law, and the responsibilities of marriage and family life (like his parents) were the expectations placed on him from an early age. His habits of working hard and respecting family life remained with him, as a result of his strict, disciplined but loving upbringing.

---

1. Luther's family name, Luder, could be spelled in a variety of ways. Luther preferred the spelling that was closest to the Greek word *eleutheros*, meaning "free," a play on words as Luther discovered the "freedom" from sin that he had through faith in Christ.

Map of Luther's Germany—key towns and regions

His schooling in Mansfeld and nearby Eisenach, from ages seven to sixteen, prepared him for university studies at Erfurt, where he lived in a hostel run under the strict principles of a monastery. This included communal prayer four times a day, chores, breakfast, private studies, etc. Martin was an able student, and graduated with excellence in the combination of studies of the Middle Ages, grammar, logic, and rhetoric *(trivium),* which prepared students for careers in law, medicine, or theology in four years, the shortest possible time.

By 1501 he had moved schools three times, and in later life felt that his teachers had been unduly harsh towards him, but in

1502 he was able to pass his baccalaureate exams in the several liberal arts of grammar, rhetoric, logic, arithmetic, geometry, music, and astronomy. Three years of further study in philosophy, logic, mathematics, and music followed. In 1505, at the age of twenty-two, he graduated second in his class of seventeen, and was ready to study the profession marked out for him by his father as the most promising for his future: law.

But despite his parents' wishes and expectations, his life would take a very different course. In 1504, just before his twenty-first birthday, he had suffered an accident with a friend's sword and sustained a serious injury. The possibility of death and coming before God's judgment terrified him. He later called this experience his *anfechtung* (trial, temptation, tribulation, or affliction), so severely was he moved by it. He felt he would die and be cast into hell as punishment for his sins. This paralyzing fear of death, judgment, and hell would traumatize him throughout his life, but particularly plagued the young Martin. An outbreak of the plague in 1505 caused the deaths of some of his fellow students, and he had moments where he could do nothing, so terrified was he of what might happen.

Then on the night of 2 July 1505, he was caught in a sudden thunderstorm on his way back to Erfurt from a visit to his parents in Mansfeld, on the road near Stottenheim. A bolt of lightning struck right beside him. His legs could feel the electric current vibrate around him. Terrified he was about to die, he vowed "Save me, St. Anna, and I will become a monk." Profoundly shaken by this Stottenheim road experience, fifteen days later he joined the Augustinian hermits of Erfurt, committing himself to a life of prayer, service and study.

So angry was his father at hearing this news, that a conflict between them began that would continue for another twenty years, when Luther was eventually, and as an outcome of his revolutionary teaching about the monastic life, to take a wife. But these thoughts were far from Luther's mind now. He devoted himself to a life of poverty, chastity, and obedience, seeking the inner peace he so longed for. However, the life of intense religious practices only made things worse. He was aware of his sinfulness. The regular practice of confessing his sins only made him feel more guilty and less forgiven. His awe of God was not met with a sense of God's love and acceptance, and once ordained as a priest and taking his first Mass, he was speechless because of his fear at being in the presence of God, and tried to run away from the service. Only a telling-off from his teacher made him continue.

Luther's understanding of God as the Almighty filled him with fear. He was anxious and miserable as he thought of having to stand before the Judge of the world and give an account of his life. So he pushed himself to study the Bible more thoroughly. Up to this time, study of the Scriptures had been primarily to justify the teaching of the church, and to illustrate the philosophical arguments of the Scholastics, men like Thomas Aquinas and Duns Scotus, who had tried to bring the teachings of the church in line with the teachings of the Greek philosophers, Plato and Aristotle. But Luther came to the Word of God looking for answers to his own personal dilemmas.

He studied the Bible in depth, learning the original languages of Greek and Hebrew, and gaining a reputation for his outstanding knowledge. Eventually, his monumental achievement of translating the Bible into the language of the common people would demonstrate his mastery of the library of books that make up the Old and New Testaments. It would become the foundation for all he would later write and teach, and his basis for argument as he challenged the authority of the Roman Catholic Church. He later wrote "The Scriptures are a vast forest, but there is not one tree in it that I have not shaken with my hand."[2]

With the invention of printing, copies of the Bible were now more available, and the young monk may have obtained his own copy. His studies in theology in Erfurt, then Wittenberg in 1508, and some time in Rome, led to him joining the theology faculty at Wittenberg and graduating as a Doctor (teacher) of Theology in 1513. He began teaching the Bible in the same year, concentrating on lectures on Genesis and Psalms. His lectures

2. Pelikan and Lehman, eds., *Luther's Works (LW)*, 54:121.

were well-prepared, and although he was not the greatest Hebrew scholar, he made copious notes on the grammar and questions of translation, and gave his students detailed notes on the theology of each section. In 1515 he moved on to Romans, and was drawn to the thought of the apostle Paul, especially his understanding of law, grace, and salvation.

Luther realized that the key problem he faced—how he could appear before the judgment of an angry God—was answered by the doctrine of justification by faith alone, and not his own works of righteousness or attempts to justify himself. The text "the just shall live by faith" transformed his life and removed his deep-seated sense of guilt, fear, and judgment. He wrote:

> I greatly longed to understand Paul's Epistle to the Romans and nothing stood in the way but that one expression, "the justice of God," because I took it to mean that justice whereby God is just and deals justly in punishing the unjust. My situation was that, although an impeccable monk, I stood before God as a sinner troubled in conscience, and I had no confidence that my merit would assuage him. Therefore I did not love a just and angry God, but rather hated and murmured against him. Yet I clung to the dear Paul and had a great yearning to know what he meant.
>
> Night and day I pondered until I saw the connection between the justice of God and the statement that "the just shall live by his faith." Then I grasped that the justice of God is that righteousness by which through grace and sheer mercy God justifies us through faith. Thereupon I felt myself to be reborn and to have gone through open doors into paradise. The whole of Scripture took on a new meaning, and whereas before the "justice of God" had filled me with hate, now it became to me inexpressibly sweet in greater love. This passage of Paul became to me a gate to heaven. . . .
>
> If you have a true faith that Christ is your Savior, then at once you have a gracious God, for faith leads you

in and opens up God's heart and will, that you should see pure grace and overflowing love. This it is to behold God in faith that you should look upon his fatherly, friendly heart, in which there is no anger nor ungraciousness. He who sees God as angry does not see him rightly but looks only on a curtain, as if a dark cloud had been drawn across his face.[3]

Teaching and Preaching

Luther's responsibilities now included preaching regularly at the church in Wittenberg, close to the castle that housed the Augustinian monastery where he lived. He became the district vicar for ten monasteries, which brought much administrative responsibility and was time consuming, but gave him detailed understanding of caring for both personal, spiritual, and pastoral needs. Many confessed to problems of sin and guilt that alienated them from God and one another. The answer for them was the sacrament of penance, which involved showing repentance (contrition), confessing their sin to a priest, and seeking absolution. On confession of their sin the priest would prescribe a series of acts of contrition to satisfy the requirements of God's justice and judgment, but often these acts were not completed, and the sinner was left lacking "satisfaction." If they died in this state they would go to purgatory, and in order to reduce the "satisfaction deficit" an indulgence could be purchased or granted, which would reduce the amount of time in purgatory.

Luther came to believe that indulgences had no effect and gave false hope. He scheduled a debate on the subject in 1517, and according to tradition posted ninety-five theses on the subject to the door of the church on about 31 October, to alert his students. Later legend has him nailing the theses to the door of the Castle Church in Wittenberg, but historians are uncertain about the accuracy of this dramatic description. It was common practice for

3. From Luther, *The Sermon on the Mount and the Magnificat* in *Luther Works* 21:37, quoted in Bainton, *Life of Luther*, 48–51.

a university lecturer to post the title and subject matter of their lecture in a public space. But what did take place nevertheless shook the palaces and cathedrals of Europe, and would change the balance of power between pope, princes, and people for all time.

Luther's ninety-five theses are provocative and polemical, challenging to debate. Article 1 states:

> When our Lord and Master Jesus Christ said; "Do penance (*penitentiam agite*) etc.," he intended that the entire life of believers should be one of repentance (*penitentiam*).[4]

Luther had discovered through reading the Greek of the passage in Matthew 4:17 that the real meaning of the passage was not "do penance," as the Latin Bible had it, but "repent"—a continuous process of changing one's mind and direction of life away from sin and back to God, a continuous conversion.

This challenged the heart of the system of penance, and with it the economic system on which the bishops and the pope depended. The theses were translated from Latin into German and 100,000 copies distributed. The authorities, Albrecht of Mainz and Pope Leo X, tried to ignore the threat, but soon turned the matter over to the papal theologian, Sylvester Mazzolini, a Dominican monk known as Prierias, who published his own attack on Luther, *Dialogue against the Theses of Martin Luther concerning the Power of the Pope.*

Prierias argued that Luther was wrong to challenge the authority of the pope, who was the head of the church, and infallible (unable to err in matters of doctrine). Anyone who challenged the pope's authority, such as in the matter of indulgences, was a heretic deserving excommunication. He summoned Luther to Rome, and sent a letter to the papal legate (ambassador) in Germany to have Luther arrested, brought to Rome, where he would be tried, found guilty, and burnt at the stake.

However, Frederick the Wise, one of the seven papal electors in Germany, had his own ambitions and plans, and came to

---

4. Pelikan and Lehman, eds., *LW*, 31:233–38

Luther's defence. His own national interests led him to allow Luther to defend himself first in Germany, as this was a local matter and Frederick did not appreciate the pope's direct interference in what he saw as a local German affair. Also, Luther's sudden fame and the publicity that had been generated put the University of Wittenberg on the map. Frederick was the founder of the university and was greatly pleased to have this rising academic star on the faculty. Only if it was absolutely necessary would Luther be handed over to the pope.

Instead Frederick arranged for a debate between Luther and papal legate Cardinal Cajetan at the upcoming diet (public meeting) of Augsburg in October 1518. Here, Luther defended himself against the accusations of heresy, and strengthened his accusations against papal authority. No compromise was reached, and Luther was dismissed from the Cardinal's presence. He fled the city and returned to Wittenberg, where he continued to teach, gain allies in the University faculty, and attract discussion. In 1519 he was invited to debate his theology at the University of Leipzig. To avoid being caught up in more controversy Luther's colleagues Andreas Bodenstein and Philip Melanchthon were given the task of defending his views against the brilliant professor of theology, Johannes Eck. But Luther was drawn in and stated that where it came to the matter of indulgences and the authority of the pope to administer them, what was most important was the relationship of the Christian to Christ himself.

Eck accused Luther of taking up the position of Jan Hus, who had been condemned as a heretic and whose followers had attacked the city of Leipzig, smearing Luther's name by association with a discredited position and a hated enemy who had been put to death in 1415, one hundred years previously.

Luther took a break from the debate to research Hus' views, which he found were not heretical, but in line with Scripture. He articulated what would become one of the key principles of the Reformation, *sola Scriptura* ("by Scripture alone"), that if pope or council disagreed with the teaching of Scripture they were wrong, whereas Hus and Luther were in agreement with Scripture. The Bible was the ultimate authority, no earthly authority or power could go against it.

Luther returned to Wittenberg more convinced of this position, and seriously concerned that the pope might be the Antichrist and the Church of Rome deceived. He wrote: "I whisper this in your ear. I cannot decide whether the Pope is the Antichrist or merely one of his chief henchmen, so violently does he deny Christ in his decretals and canons."[5]

Eck considered he had won the debate by forcing Luther to declare his opposition to the authority of the pope, and began to prepare the bull (papal document) of excommunication of Luther.

In 1520, Luther's thirty-seventh year, he wrote three important treatises that would mark out his theological position, set the course of the Reformation, and change the map of Europe into a patchwork of Protestant and Catholic states. His *Address to the Christian Nobility of the German Nation,* dedicated to the new Holy Roman emperor, Charles V, made the radical call to German nobles to meet the emergency situation of the pope's refusal to reform its sinful, corrupt, and unbiblical practices by using their positions in society to act. They should call for a church-wide council to change church practices in their territories so as to end abuses, such as indulgences, and base teaching firmly in the Scriptures. Luther called on secular leaders to be involved in church decisions—a radical new step that again challenged the pope's claim to have authority over political powers—and to take responsibility to see that the teaching of the church was in line with the Bible.

The pope prepared his own counter-attack, and on 10 June issued the bull *Exsurge Domine* ("Arise O Lord"), condemning Luther's teaching as heretical, banning his works, and giving him sixty days to withdraw his previous writings and return to the church. The bull reached Luther on 10 October in Wittenberg, and he quickly fired back a Latin response (and German translation) aptly titled *Adversus Execrabilem Antichristi bullam* ("Against the Execrable Bull of the Antichrist").

5. Kittelson, "Luther and Modern Church History," 262.

Luther's other two majors work of that year, *On the Babylonian Captivity of the Church* and *The Freedom of a Christian,*
brought together a summary of his criticisms of the Church of
Rome: the seven sacraments, the medieval system of administering
God's grace to the Christian, were all corrupted by papal authority.

Luther charged that it was wrong to withhold the communion cup from the laity and reserve it for those ordained to the
priesthood. In Scripture, Jesus invites *all* to both eat and drink of
his body and blood. But again, the doctrine of transubstantiation
and the idea that the Mass was a repetition of Christ's sacrifice on
the cross were also in error when compared with what Scripture
taught.

Luther dedicated *The Freedom of a Christian* to Pope Leo X,
even though the threat of execution overshadowed him. The treatise is a calm and measured statement of his beliefs, and whilst the
pope was not likely to change his mind on the excommunication,
Luther's approach is that of reasoned persuasion. The Christian, he
argues, from Paul's paradox in the Letter to the Romans, chapter
7, is *both* bound *and* free. He is bound to be subject of all, but he is
set free from the tyranny of the (Old Testament) law and from the
fear of eternal damnation.

Confrontation at Worms

Luther published *The Freedom of a Christian* in November 1520,
and on 10 December the pope's sixty-day period to recant expired.
His books had been publicly burned in Cologne and Mainz as heresy, and now Luther took the bold step of burning books of Roman
Catholic doctrine, including *Exsurge Domine*, the Pope's condemnation of Luther. The pope responded by formally excommunicat-
ing Luther on 3 January 1521, declaring Luther a heretic, subject
to immediate arrest and trial. But Frederick had other plans, and
rather than handing Luther over to the papal authorities, summoned him to another diet (formal meeting) at Worms, some 300
miles from Wittenberg, to receive a fair hearing for his views.

Luther arrived in Worms at the head of a triumphant procession of his supporters on 16 April. Before an assembly of the emperor, his nobles, the bishops, cardinals, and abbots, all ceremoniously dressed, Luther was overawed. His opponent in the previous debate, Eck, asked if he was finally willing to recant of the teachings in the large pile of his books which were placed on the central table. Luther hesitated, and asked for a day to consider. The night gave him time to think and ponder his situation. He wrote out his response and memorized it. The next day he returned, placed the books in three piles, and spoke about them.

The first pile contained moral teachings and Christian reflections on piety that no one would have any quarrel with. The second group contained his controversial works about the abuses of the clergy and the pope. He would not recant on these, as the corrupt practices were ongoing. The third pile contained his most vitriolic and personal attacks on individuals, which he now regretted expressing in such terms and tone, but nevertheless upheld the theological truths he had articulated.

His speech, both in Latin and then in German, appeared conciliatory, but gave no concessions, and Eck again demanded that he recant, asking sarcastically if Luther thought he was the only one who could understand Scripture's teaching. Luther replied with four now-famous sentences:

> Unless I am convinced by the testimony of the Scriptures or by clear reason (for I do not trust either in the Pope or in councils alone, since it is well known that they have often erred and contradicted themselves), I am bound by the Scriptures I have quoted and my conscience is captive to the Word of God. I cannot and I will not retract anything, since it is neither safe nor right to go against conscience. I cannot do otherwise, here I stand, may God help me. Amen.[6]

The next day the young Charles V, the Holy Roman emperor, gave a speech declaring Luther a heretic, and stated his intention of wiping out Luther's innovations. But he allowed him safe conduct

6. Whitford, *Guide*, 43.

back to Wittenberg. A month later the Edict of Worms was published, stating that any who helped Luther would also be treated as heretics, to be handed over to the imperial authorities for trial and punishment, most likely execution.

However, Frederick the Wise offered Luther protection by hiding him. While still on the road from Worms to Wittenberg Luther was apprehended by armed men who took him by force from his companions and, once out of view, released him. Luther went to the castle fortress at Wartburg, disguised himself by growing a beard and letting his hair grow, and lived in a small room above the commander, who protected him and kept his presence secret.

In Hiding

Luther was far from idle in the eleven months he stayed in Warburg. He translated the New Testament from Greek into the common language of the people, German. It took him three months to translate, but his translation, the equivalent of the King James version in English, is a monument to his skill as a translator, and also a literary masterpiece that helped to standardize German as a language and has permeated German life and culture ever since. In many churches today Luther's translation is the version that is used.

In March 1522 Luther left his hiding to attend to the chaotic situation in Wittenberg. Disputes over celebrating the Eucharist by giving both bread and wine to the ordinary people, wandering prophets proclaiming the end times, and his colleague Andreas von Karlstad declaring his intention to marry and renounce his monastic vows, produced a situation of riots, anarchy, and vandalism. Luther immediately preached a series of eight sermons over eight days to calm the frenzy. His message was on the need for charity with one another, and the need to make reforms not through acts of violence or imposing new laws by force, but through persuasion. The gospel should not be transformed into a new law, for "faith must come freely without compulsion."[7]

7. Ibid., 48.

Order was restored, and Luther settled back in to writing and teaching, preparing the treatises on Christian life and organizing the University. But other challenges lay before him. In 1525 Luther took the step of marriage. Nine nuns had come to Wittenberg the previous November, where they had renounced their vows and Luther had tried to find them marriage partners. One remained, Katherina von Bora (1499–1552). Luther thought the idea of marrying her ridiculous, but his father advised it, and they went ahead, more to anger the pope than out of romantic love. But over time their relationship grew into a deep and loving commitment, and six children were born, four of whom lived beyond childhood.

Controversies and Creeds

In 1525 Luther also was in conflict with one of his former friends and allies against Rome, the humanist and scholar Desiderius Erasmus. Luther was influenced by Erasmus' care for and love of the Scriptures, but they disagreed over the place of free will, and he severed ties with the scholar, although it would have been politically expedient for him to have maintained their collaborative relationship. Had Luther continued in friendly correspondence with Erasmus, his own learning and study of the Scripture might have assumed a less dogmatic and at times vitriolic tone, as Erasmus, a harbinger of careful study and moderate views, influenced many of the Reformers to defend the values of human reason and compassion for humanity. Unfortunately, Luther parted company with one of the few intellectual giants of the time who could have held him to account for some of his more extreme views.

Luther's concerns were not primarily academic or based in the world of scholarship, but in the practical realities of pastoring and teaching those for whom he had spiritual responsibility and pastoral oversight. He realized through visiting his parishioners that the debates he had been having with the church authorities needed to be plainly explained, and produced *The Small Catechism*, a manual of basic Christian discipleship and instruction for families and parish clergy, with short, easily memorable answers to key questions about the Christian faith. Here are his short comments on the Ten Commandments:

The Ten Commandments

As the head of the family should teach them in a simple way to his household.

> The First Commandment: Thou shalt have no other gods.

What does this mean? We should fear, love, and trust in God above all things.

> The Second Commandment: Thou shalt not take the name of the Lord, thy God, in vain.

What does this mean? We should fear and love God that we may not curse, swear, use witchcraft, lie, or deceive by His name, but call upon it in every trouble, pray, praise, and give thanks.

> The Third Commandment: Thou shalt sanctify the holy day.

What does this mean? We should fear and love God that we may not despise preaching and His Word, but hold it sacred, and gladly hear and learn it.

> The Fourth Commandment: Thou shalt honor thy father and thy mother [that it may be well with thee and thou mayest live long upon the earth].

What does this mean? We should fear and love God that we may not despise nor anger our parents and masters, but give them honor, serve, obey, and hold them in love and esteem.

> The Fifth Commandment: Thou shalt not kill.

What does this mean? We should fear and love God that we may not hurt nor harm our neighbor in his body, but help and befriend him in every bodily need [in every need and danger of life and body].

The Sixth Commandment: Thou shalt not commit adultery.

What does this mean? We should fear and love God that we may lead a chaste and decent life in words and deeds, and each love and honor his spouse.

The Seventh Commandment: Thou shalt not steal.

What does this mean? We should fear and love God that we may not take our neighbor's money or property, nor get them by false ware or dealing, but help him to improve and protect his property and business [that his means are preserved and his condition is improved].

The Eighth Commandment: Thou shalt not bear false witness against thy neighbor.

What does this mean? We should fear and love God that we may not deceitfully belie, betray, slander, or defame our neighbor, but defend him, [think and] speak well of him, and put the best construction on everything.

The Ninth Commandment: Thou shalt not covet thy neighbor's house.

What does this mean? We should fear and love God that we may not craftily seek to get our neighbor's inheritance or house, and obtain it by a show of [justice and] right, etc., but help and be of service to him in keeping it.

The Tenth Commandment: Thou shalt not covet thy neighbor's wife, nor his man-servant, nor his maid-servant, nor his cattle, nor anything that is his.

What does this mean? We should fear and love God that we may not estrange, force, or entice away our neighbor's wife, servants, or cattle, but urge them to stay and [diligently] do their duty.

What does God say of all these commandments?

He says thus (Exod. 20:5f): I the Lord, thy God, am a jealous God, visiting the iniquity of the fathers upon the children unto the third and fourth generation of them that hate Me, and showing mercy unto thousands of them that love Me and keep My commandments.

What does this mean? God threatens to punish all that transgress these commandments. Therefore we should dread His wrath and not act contrary to these commandments. But He promises grace and every blessing to all that keep these commandments. Therefore we should also love and trust in Him, and gladly do [zealously and diligently order our whole life] according to His commandments.[8]

The Large Catechism was designed for educated pastors to give more detailed explanations of the fundamentals of the faith.

The Birth of Protestantism

Luther's reforms were still in danger of suppression by the Roman Catholic Church. In 1529 the Diet of Speyer met to enforce the Edict of Worms which had been temporarily suspended. However, six German princes and fourteen imperial cities under the Holy Roman Empire issued a formal protest (*Protestatio,* from which we get the term "Protestant") to Emperor Charles V. This gave the "protestants" time to organize, for Luther's allies to organize themselves, and for Luther to consolidate his theological positions.

Political events galvanized the Protestant German rulers into action. The Turks attacked Vienna in October 1529, and Emperor Charles V needed to rely on the support of all German citizens, even those following Luther and his Reformation principles of justification by faith and refusal to accept the authority of the pope. He asked the rulers to summarize their positions, and they produced, with Luther's help, the *Augsburg Confession.* This document, carefully written by Philip Melanchthon, Luther's colleague at Wittenberg, dealt with the complicated issues of how Christians

8. Luther, *Small Catechism*, 538–40.

should fulfill their duties within the state, serving public order and secular state, even with a monarch loyal to the Church of Rome. They could thus cooperate and serve together in the army to defeat the threat of the Ottoman Empire at their gates.

But the Protestant states still felt under threat from the Holy Roman emperor, and formed the Schmalkaldic League, with Luther's support and encouragement. The League existed not only to support the empire against external threats, but also to maintain religious diversity within it. Luther also wrote a *Warning to His Dear German Nation,* which was published in 1530, and again in the 1540s when a war broke out between the emperor and the League.

Luther's writing and sermons continued. There were now eighty-five volumes of his materials, and his lectures on Genesis and Romans bedded in many of his key doctrines as he gave expositions on Scripture. Amidst the many publications of this time, *On the Jews and the Lies* was an anti-Semitic diatribe filled with hatred and polemic against the Jewish people, and we shall focus on this in chapter 4.

Luther's Death

Luther had suffered various illnesses from his youth, which he often ascribed to attacks of the devil. From his forties he had angina attacks, with intense pain, from the clogging of the arteries in the heart. On 1 February 1546 at the age of sixty-two, whilst walking 100 kilometers to Eisleben, he had a heart attack, the first of several over the next few weeks. He was overcome with pain, and passed out.

In his final weeks he preached a series of sermons, to which he added *Admonition against the Jews* (7 February 1546), advocating the expulsion of the Jews from Germany if they did not accept conversion to Christianity. We will examine this below.

A week later, on 17 February, he had another attack, and went to bed. Later that night, he suffered a final attack. His assistant Justus Jonas prayed with him by his bedside, and asked him: "Reverend Father, are you ready to die trusting in your Lord Jesus

Christ and to confess [affirm] the doctrine which you have taught in his name?" Luther answered "Yes" and then died. Rather than receiving the Last Rites or giving a final confession of his sins as in the Roman Catholic Church, Luther died affirming his beliefs in the power of God to save, and in the hope of the resurrection of the dead.

His body was taken back to Wittenberg and on 22 February the community mourned his death and witnessed to his faith. His friend and pastor of the city church Johannes Bugenhagen took the service, and Melanchthon gave the tribute. Luther was buried beneath the pulpit of the Castle Church, from which he had preached the Word of God for some forty years, and shook the world. It was a fitting resting place, and can still be seen today by the millions of tourists who visit Wittenberg each year.

1517–1660: The Reformation

Lutheranism spread throughout northern Europe in the sixteenth century, especially in Scandinavia and the Baltic countries. The Reformation continued throughout the sixteenth and seventeenth centuries, and the Roman Catholic Church responded with the Counter-Reformation, defining its doctrine at a series of councils, the best known being the Council of Trent between 1545 and 1563.

Here the Roman Catholic Church condemned the principles and doctrines of Luther and the Reformers, some of Luther's contributions, and strengthened its own powers and administrative efficiency to deal with heresy.

The council reaffirmed the creeds, and also the writings of the Apocrypha, which Luther had placed in a separate section of his translation of the Bible, and said were not as inspired as the Old and New Testaments. The official Latin translation, the Vulgate, was to be used, rather than Luther's translation in German, as the authoritative version of Scripture.

The council pronounced on the other differences with Luther. Justification by faith had also to be accompanied by human action rather than by being passively received, and it was "vain confidence" for the Reformers simply to put their trust in God's ability to save, rather than taking responsibility for their own actions. The Protestants were also in error to think that the grace of God could not be lost through mortal sin. Such discussions continue today between Protestants and Roman Catholics, but much misunderstanding has been clarified, and increasingly Christians of all denominations affirm the common ground between them rather than heighten their differences.

The Council of Trent affirmed the seven sacraments—baptism, communion, marriage, penance, ordination, last unction, ordination (whereas the Lutherans affirmed only baptism and communion, though some affirmed penance/absolution), including the nature of the Eucharist as a transubstantiation of the bread and wine into the body and blood of Christ.

Priestly ordination, according to Trent, was in succession to the Levitical priesthood of the Old Testament, and under the authority of the apostles and their successors. The doctrines of purgatory, indulgences, prayer through the saints, and the importance of relics, were also re-emphasized. The council prepared a list of forbidden books (*Index Librorum Prohibitorum*) which would include the works of Luther, Calvin, and the other Reformers. An alternative catechism was also entrusted to Pope Pius IV, who issued a papal bull, *Benedictus Deus* ("Blessed Be God") on 26 January 1564, which anathematized those who did not accept the decrees of the council, and appointed a commission of cardinals to put the decrees into practice.

The Catholic rulers of France, Spain, the Netherlands, Italy, Portugal, and Poland accepted the decrees, and those princes of Germany loyal to the pope accepted them at the Diet of Augsburg in 1566.

The course of European history was greatly impacted by the Reformation. The Thirty Years' War (1618–48) between Catholic and Protestant rulers weakened the Holy Roman Empire, confining it to Germany and Austria. Lutherans shaped the political map of Europe and the theological controversies of a divided Christendom in the centuries that followed.

Lutherans Today

Today there are more than 80 million Lutherans worldwide, the third largest grouping of Protestant churches, after Anglicans and Pentecostals. The Lutheran World Federation represents some 72 million, with a further 8 million in smaller organizations. Germany has the largest number, approximately 12 million, with some 6 million in Sweden, Ethiopia, Tanzania, and Indonesia. The USA and Norway have about 4 million, and UK approximately 200,000. Luther himself did not like the term "Lutheran," preferring to call himself and others who affirmed the gospel "evangelical." Today this term has different meanings in different contexts, but for Luther it meant those who stood by the good news of Jesus Christ, and recognized the need for Reformation in the church.

Luther did not intend to form a new church or denomination, but rather to remain within the "one, holy, catholic, and apostolic church" (the four marks of the church, according to the Nicene Creed). His followers, and those of the other Reformers—John Calvin and Huldrych Zwingli in Switzerland, Thomas Cranmer in England, John Knox in Scotland, and many others—wanted to restore a biblical foundation to the church based on the three solas: *sola Scriptura, sola gratia, sola fide* ("by Scripture alone, by grace alone, by faith alone").

Following the death of Luther in 1546, there were three main developments over the centuries, which we need to know about in order to understand his legacy today. These were Protestant Orthodoxy/Scholasticism (sixteenth to seventeenth centuries), Enlightenment Rationalism (eighteenth to nineteenth centuries) and Pietism (eighteenth to nineteenth centuries).

Like the Scholastics ("school men") of the Middle Ages in the Roman Catholic Church, such as Thomas Aquinas, who focused his energies on discussion of the philosophical nature of Christianity, the Protestant Scholastics focused on correctly interpreting Luther's theology. The focus shifted from the experience of salvation by grace through faith to deciding what correct doctrine was, and this meant understanding the relationship between law and grace, and the place of good works. Melanchthon, Luther's colleague and disciple, mediated between conflicting views, and decided that although good works were not necessary to earn salvation, they were still necessary in the life of a believer.

Other matters under discussion were the relationship of the church to the state, the place of free will, and the way in which Jesus was present in the sacrament of communion. Different factions arose, but Melanchthon was again able to unite most of them by re-affirming the *Augsburg Confession*, which stated that in the bread and the wine the body and blood of Jesus were "truly present" without necessarily inferring that the bread and wine had been "transubstantiated."

These logical debates seem like hair-splitting today, but the different Lutheran sects continued to have differences. This was followed by the Rationalist movement of the eighteenth century, arising from the Enlightenment. Rationalism now became a force that opposed religion and imposed its own views on the nature of progress, the perfectibility of human nature, and the supremacy of human reason over faith. The Rationalists used scientific method to challenge the inspiration and authority of the Bible, disputed the evidence for miracles and the supernatural, and questioned the existence of God.

Lutherans were not against the use of reason, but saw faith in God as the starting point for reason. This discussion would be solved in various ways, with some Lutherans relying solely on faith, others on reason, and somewhere in between.

In reaction to the arid rationalism of some Lutherans and philosophers such as Gottfried Leibniz and Immanuel Kant, Philip Spener (1635–1705) and August Franke (1663–1727) pioneered a movement of revival and personal piety within the Lutheran Church. They formed groups to meet together for Bible study and prayer, calling them *collegia pietatis* ("associations of piety"), and were known as "Pietists." The practical effects in the lives of believers of such studies were increased evangelism, mission, and social concern.

One of the Pietists, Count Zinzendorf (1700–1760), formed a community on his estate in Moravia, offering refuge from persecution to the disciples of Jan Hus, whose works Luther had studied and linked to his own. Pietism renewed the training of Lutheran pastors through the University of Halle.

Lutherans in Norway, Sweden, Finland, Iceland, and Denmark consolidated into national churches and became the official state church in Denmark, Sweden, and Finland. There were few splits or divisions compared with Protestant churches founded by other Reformers. Lutherans in the USA formed several synods, some more evangelical than others.

In the 1930s, however, the Lutheran church was in league with Hitler and the Nazis in promoting the link between Lutheranism and German culture, and in developing the anti-Semitic tradition that Luther had championed. While Lutherans in Denmark and Norway resisted this, the German Lutherans re-printed Luther's sermons as part of their propaganda, and proclaimed with pride that *Kristallnacht*—the destruction of Jewish homes and property, and the burning of synagogues—took place on 10 November 1938, the anniversary of Luther's birthday.

The bishop of the Evangelical Lutheran Church in Thuringia, Martin Sasse, was a leading member of the Nazi German Christians, the national body of churches that supported the Nazis. He published a compendium of Martin Luther's writings shortly after *Kristallnacht*. In it he "applauded the burning of the synagogues" and the coincidence of the day, writing in the introduction, "On 10 November 1938, on Luther's birthday, the synagogues are burning in Germany." The German people, he urged, ought to heed these words "of the greatest anti-Semite of his time, the warner of his people against the Jews." Luther's 1543 pamphlet, *On the Jews and Their Lies,* had been the blueprint for the *Kristallnacht*.[9]

Only a few Lutheran Christians resisted the Nazis in Germany, including Pastors Martin Niemöller (1892–1984) and Dietrich Bonhoeffer (1906–45), the latter who was arrested and executed for his part in the plot to assassinate Hitler.

9. MacCulloch, *Reformation: Europe's House Divided,* 666–67.

Conclusion

The life of Luther, with all its drama, reveals a larger-than-life character caught up in the powerful forces of his day. His impact would change the world of the Middle Ages, held in the powerful grip of church and state, into the beginnings of the modern world as we know it today. Luther was the catalyst for revolutions, not just in religious faith, but in modern politics, the rise of nations and nationalism, the development of the German language through his Bible translation, and the daily life of people in education, society, and government.

His greatest achievement, or discovery, was that he was loved by God through Jesus Christ, who died on the cross and rose from the dead so his sins might be forgiven and his guilt taken away. It is thus ironic that Luther's greatest error (of which—as a man of flawed words, character, and deeds—there were many) was to accuse the Jewish people, whose Messiah he acknowledged as Savior and Lord, of being the enemies of God, and to make them his own enemies, despite their innocence, inability to defend themselves against his attacks, and the testimony of the Scriptures that he upheld. But who were the Jewish people, and how did Luther then, and how do we today, understand their significance and role? We turn to this in the next chapter.

CHAPTER 2

Who Are the Jewish people?

Jewish History

WHENEVER MY FAMILY SIT down for our Passover Seder (meal and service), there is always a great sense of history. We say together the words "My father was a wandering Aramean," referring to Abraham, who wandered from Ur in modern-day Iraq to Canaan and Egypt, living the life of a nomad some 4,000 years ago. Jewish people see him not only as their common ancestor, but have also seen each generation as in some way following in his footsteps as a wandering people, ever faced with exile from their homeland in Israel, and looking for the promise of return. As Jewish people, we have long memories, and our history reminds us continually of our survival as a people, often in hostile environments, and of our need to rely on divine protection and preservation.

Luther appeared on the scene at a time when Europe was emerging from the Middle Ages into the modern world. Christianity had existed for some 1,500 years, but was based in the Scriptures, the writings of the Jewish people, who had walked the sands of modern-day Iraq and Israel some 1,000 years before the birth of Christ. When Luther took aim at the Jewish people, and wrote scathing denunciations of their beliefs, methods of interpreting Scripture, attitudes to Jesus, and their general life and character in the Germany of his day, he was repeating the accusations and anti-Semitism of millennia, and amplifying them with his own special brand of invective, scathing and lewd humor, and angry attack.

So who are the Jewish people, and why did they meet with such bitter and unfair treatment?

I prefer to use the term "Jewish people," rather than "the Jews." Although the term "the Jews" is common, I often feel it generalizes and stereotypes us into one particular group, whereas the term "Jewish people" emphasizes that Jewish people are not all the same, and are not like some museum exhibit that can be pointed out as an obsolete historical curiosity.

The history of the Jewish people can be divided into seven overlapping periods, which we will briefly trace. First, the origins of ancient Israel can be traced from the call of Abraham around 1800 BCE (Before the Common Era) to the exile in Babylon in 586 BCE. The second period sees the development of the religion of Judaism, often in exile, from the return to Jerusalem in 530 BCE to the completion of the Talmud, in 500 CE (the Common Era). The third period, in which Luther lived, is that of the Jews in Christian Europe and Moslem Spain, from 500 to 1492. The fourth stage is from the medieval ghettos of Europe, and the opening of the New World, to the French revolution in 1789. The fifth period, of emancipation, continues from 1800 until the Holocaust of 1939. The sixth period covers the Holocaust itself, and the seventh, the reestablishment of the State of Israel, until the present day. In each of these seven periods the Jewish people were but a small number of the world's population, often on the margins of larger empires and peoples, yet through their continued survival and contribution to wider society they have had a lasting and significant impact on the whole world.

"How odd of God to choose the Jews": The Origins of Israel

First, the origins of ancient Israel, from the call of Abraham in 1800 BCE to the exile in Babylon in 586 BCE.

The Bible tells how the call of Abraham came unexpectedly and inconveniently to a prosperous Mesopotamian merchant who left his home in Ur (in Northern Iraq) to become a migrant wandering in the Middle East in search of a permanent home. His family settled in Canaan for a few generations, then sought refuge in nearby Egypt to escape famine. The stay in Egypt lasted longer than expected and, after 400 years of slavery, Moses led the mixed group of Hebrew slaves back across the Sinai desert toward Canaan. En route they camped at Mount Sinai, where Moses received a series of commandments that the Israelites were to put into practice when they entered the land of Canaan.

Around the year 1220 BCE the Israelites under Joshua entered the land of Canaan, and won victories over the native inhabitants that enabled them to capture Canaanite cities and set up their own tribal territories. The twelve tribes were independent, but united for military defence, especially against the Canaanites who remained on the land, and the Philistines, the sea peoples from the Aegean islands of ancient Greece. A series of impromptu leaders known as judges (with executive and military power) rose to power, but without a king, lawlessness and anarchy broke out, as "everyone did what was right in their own eyes" (Judg 21:25).

Around the year 1090 BCE the tribal confederacy merged into a monarchy. The first three kings—Saul, David, and Solomon—united the people, setting up a central government and place of worship in Jerusalem, and building an empire. But after the death of Solomon the monarchy split, with the ten tribes of the north setting up their own king, priesthood, and calendar, while the two southern tribes, Judah and Benjamin, remained loyal to the dynasty of David and looked for it to one day unite the tribes again. The ideal was not realized, and within the next 200 years the northern kingdom was swallowed up by the Assyrians (722 BCE) and their successors, the Babylonians under Nebuchadnezzar, captured Jerusalem, destroying the temple and taking into exile the leaders of the population of Judah (586 BCE).

The Development of Judaism:
530 BCE–500 CE

The second period sees the development of the religion of Judaism, often in exile, from the return to Jerusalem in 530 BCE to the completion of the Talmud, in 500 CE.

The history of the Jewish people is one of exile and return, and what seemed a disaster became an opportunity for the spread of the Jewish people around the ancient world (*Diaspora* = "scattering"), the consolidation of their faith through the implementing of the laws of Moses, and the development of their understanding of the universal claims of their God to be the one true God over all nations, and not just a tribal deity. While some exiles returned under the benevolent policies of Cyrus the Persian in 530 BCE, many remained in exile, and prospered there.

Those who returned, such as Ezra and Nehemiah, faced the hard task of repairing the walls of Jerusalem, rebuilding the temple, ridding the people of pagan practices and non-Israelite wives, and eking out a survival in the midst of poor harvests and foreign powers.

A succession of Greek, Roman, and Christian rulers over the next 500 years were the context for further transformations. When the temple, rebuilt by Herod the Great as a monstrous display of his wealth and power, was again destroyed by the Roman legions of Titus and Vespasian in 70 CE, the rabbis, the successors of the priests of Israel, consolidated the system of law and set up their own academies, dynasties, and authority. The oral law, which according to tradition had been given to Moses on Sinai at the same time as the written law, was codified in the Mishnah (c. 220 CE) and Talmud (in Palestine, 450 CE and Babylon 550 CE), a vast series of volumes of Jewish law, literature, legend, and advice for living. "Turn it over, and turn it over again, there is everything in it."[1]

Around this time, many false messiahs appeared claiming to set the people free from their oppressors, including Bar Kochba, whose failed revolt against Rome in 132 CE finally ended Jewish

---

1. Herford, *Pirkei Abot*, 145.

possession of their capital city, Jerusalem, for 1,900 years. All these messiahs failed, but the Galilean disciples of one, a certain Yeshua ha-Notsri, claimed to have seen him risen from the grave after his crucifixion as a common criminal under the oppressive Roman laws. Not many followed him, but those who did were eventually known as "Christians," who launched their own brand of Judaism with Jesus at the center and without requiring non-Jews who joined with them to keep the Jewish laws of circumcision, the Sabbath, and the food laws.

The religion of the Jews became that of the synagogue—a place of study, prayer, and the community meeting place—in the Greco-Roman and Asian world full of gods and goddesses, Greek philosophy, Roman power, and international trade through the trade routes across Europe, Africa, and Asia. The Jews, banished from Jerusalem, were scattered across diverse nations, learning their languages, adopting their cultures, but retaining their own ethnic and religious identity, using Hebrew in the synagogue, Aramaic in the home, Greek in the market place, and Latin in the courts.

Some Jews turned to mysticism, withdrawing from the material world and searching out the mysteries of creation and redemption from a spiritual exile from true holiness that mirrored their exile from their land, holy city, and temple. Others followed the complex legal debates of the rabbis, and developed the teaching of the Talmud into a lifetime of study, prayer, and good deeds. Others embraced the growing knowledge of the Western world, delving into Greek philosophy, engaging in the world of business, politics, medicine, and the arts. Still others looked for a messiah to restore the tribes, bring them back from exile, and set up an earthly kingdom with a new Davidic king reigning from Jerusalem.

Christian Europe

The third period, that in which Luther lived, is that of the Jews in Christian Europe and Moslem Spain, from 500 to 1492.

Scattered across Europe, the Middle East, North Africa, and as far off as India and China, the Jewish people were vital to the civilizations in which they lived. While the Roman Catholic Church prevented Christians from lending to each other with interest, the Jews were required to do so at the behest of church and king, who could always confiscate their lands and property and expel them if the need arose or their own debts to the Jews became too high.

A series of expulsions occurred throughout Europe, beginning with Germany in the 1100s, and followed by England (1290), France (1306), Germany at the time of the Black Death, where the Jews were accused of poisoning the wells (1348), a charge Luther repeated, Spain (1492), in the year that Columbus set sail for America, and Portugal (1497). Blood libels—the accusation that Jews kidnapped, murdered, and used the blood of Christian children for their Passover sacrifices—sprung up in Norwich (1144), Gloucester (1168), Bury St. Edmunds (1181), Bristol (1183), Lincoln (1255), and in more than 150 places in Europe. The last recorded blood libel was in Damascus in 1840. Luther himself believed in and refers to the well-known case of Simon of Trent, a child who was allegedly kidnapped and murdered by Jews in 1475, and who was later canonized.[2] Luther repeated such accusations and used them to urge the expulsion of Jews from German cities in the 1540s.

---

2 According to historian Ronnie Po-chia Hsia: "On Easter Sunday 1475, the dead body of a 2-year-old Christian boy named Simon was found in the cellar of a Jewish family's house in Trent, Italy. Town magistrates arrested eighteen Jewish men and five Jewish women on the charge of ritual murder—the killing of a Christian child in order to use his blood in Jewish religious rites. In a series of interrogations that involved liberal use of judicial torture, the magistrates obtained the confessions of the Jewish men. Eight were executed in late June, and another committed suicide in jail." Hsia, *Trent 1475*, 178.

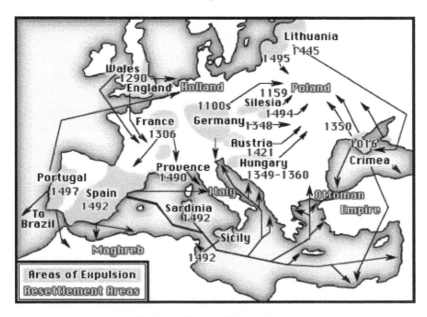

Christian Europe, Moslem Spain

In between the bouts of violence, charges of ritual murder, and expulsions, the Jewish people often lived at peace with their neighbors. Nowhere was this more so than in Moslem Spain, where in the twelfth century the great philosopher and theologian Moses Maimonides (1135–1204) was also court physician and political adviser to the Sultan. He pioneered the development of medicine, and also bridged the philosophy of Aristotle with the sacred texts of the Bible and the rabbis. Maimonides was a rationalist, who played down the supernatural aspects of the Bible and tried to interpret the description of God having feelings or parts of a body as a human way (anthropomorphism) of describing God's abstract qualities and being, a similar approach to that of his Christian and Moslem near contemporaries, Thomas Aquinas (1225–74) and Al-Gazali (1058–1111).

But despite the enlightened rationalism of scholars, who read each other's works, translated them for their students, and cooperated in the search for new knowledge, at the popular level, and in the eyes of monarchs and church leaders, the Jews remained a danger and a threat. The blood libel, the suspicion of Jews as outsiders, Christ-killers, and subverters of Christian Europe, fuelled the anti-Jewish massacres and expulsions that were a by-product of the Crusades, military campaigns to free Jerusalem and the Holy Land from Turks and Jews. The first Crusade in 1095 unleashed a wave of violence against Jewish communities throughout Europe. The word *pogrom*[3] was coined in Russia in the nineteenth century to describe the similar ransacking, looting, rape, massacres, and expulsions that victimized Jewish communities in Russia and Poland. The Crusaders were no different in their misplaced Christian zeal. There were five Crusades up to 1221, seven up to 1250, and many more minor crusades up to 1456.

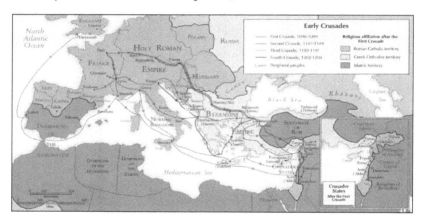

The Crusades

Throughout this period, the Jewish people were subjected to forced sermons designed to convert them, anti-Jewish legislation restricting their freedoms, and the disputation as a means of proving the truth of Christianity and refuting Jewish claims. The most important disputation was held in Barcelona in 1263 between Dominican friar Paulo Christiani and Rabbi Nachmanides, at the palace of King James I of Aragon. The debate was about whether

3. A noun from the Russian verb "to destroy, to wreak havoc, to demolish violently."

the Messiah had already come and tried to prove from the writings of the rabbis themselves that Jesus was the Messiah. The attempt failed, or rather, both sides claimed the victory, which led to the banishment of Rabbi Nachman from Spain, authority given to Christiani to force the Jews to listen to his sermons, and the burning of twenty-four wagon loads of the Talmud on the streets of Paris shortly after.

The Ghettos of Europe, and the Opening of the New World, until the French Revolution in 1789

The first *ghetto* (meaning "slag" or waste from an iron foundry) was an area of Venice where Jews were locked in at night and restrictions on their rights, access, and homes were enforced from 1516. Christian leaders followed this example, and Jewish communities throughout Europe were kept under curfew, lock and key, in the cities and regions in which they lived. But the times were changing in Europe, and the invention of printing (in which Jews were at the forefront), the renewal of knowledge from ancient Greece and Rome, the beginnings of modern science, international trade, voyages of discovery, and the independent entrepreneurial spirit of the Reformation allowed Jewish people to be more involved than previously in the contexts in which they lived. Synagogues and places of Jewish learning grew, with Jews happily coexisting alongside their neighbors in many parts of Europe.

In Poland, where the lot of the Jews as middle men between the peasants and the nobility meant they were often tax collectors, money lenders, and estate managers for absentee landlords, the need for redemption from massacre and oppression grew. A false messiah, Shabbetai Zvi, led a band of followers in a failed revolt against Christians and Muslims in 1665. While Shabbetai chose to convert to Islam rather than be put to death by the Sultan of Turkey, his followers continued to believe in him, and other false messiahs, such as Jacob Frank, found a following among Jews in Poland and Eastern Europe, and even some Christians. He became a Roman Catholic, but of a heretical kind. His movement, linked to a romantic notion of Polish nationalism, fed into the growing desire for independence from kings and states.

In England, the Jews were welcomed back from their expulsion of 1290 some 360 years later, in 1655, when Manesseh ben Israel, a Jew from Holland, petitioned Oliver Cromwell to remove the restriction on Jews living in England, and groups from Holland, Germany, and later Russia and Poland, settled back in the Britain over the next few centuries. In other countries they increasingly received rights and protection, and in the newly discovered colonies in North and South America, Africa, and Asia, they brought trade and administrative skills. The banking and financial systems that were needed to enable international trade were conducted by family businesses such as the Rothschilds, whose network of contacts allowed them up-to-date information on currencies, shipping, and political situations.

Philosophers such as Spinoza, who was banned from the synagogue in Amsterdam on the charge of atheism, but was really a scientific rationalist who believed God was in everything, was another example of the Jewish people contributing to the humanism and rationalism of the age. Whilst secular thinking separated church and state and developed the idea of rights and freedom for all, the Jews still suffered under the centuries-old prejudice against them, especially within the churches. But their situation was improving, and the following stage, emancipation, increased their freedoms to participate in wider society still more.

Felix Mendelssohn, the composer, was the grandson of Moses Mendelssohn, (1729–86), a Jewish philosopher, playwright, and theologian who developed Reform Judaism, a Judaism for the modern world that, like the emerging liberal Christianity, downplayed the supernatural and the appeal to sacred Scripture, and put forward a vision of human development that united all faiths in the search for modernity. Reform Jews had synagogues where the women could sit together with men, there was musical accompaniment with an organ, and it was not necessary to keep the Jewish law so strictly.

Emancipation Continues until the Holocaust of 1939

Emancipation brought Jews the rights to live as free citizens throughout Europe, freedoms they were quick to embrace. In varying degrees and at different rates of change in different countries, Jews were given access to education, law, government office, and allowed to pursue trades and professions previously closed to them. Their synagogues could worship in public and with legal protection. They had access to education, much of which was secular.

Many chose to be baptized, some for genuine reasons of faith, but others for admission to secular education and professions, and to marry non-Jews in Christian ceremonies. Felix Mendelssohn, the German composer, and most of his family, became Christians, contributing through his music to the cultural life of Germany, and reviving the performances of great composers, such as Bach's *St. Matthew Passion.*

Another such example was Benjamin Disraeli, Prime Minister of the United Kingdom, whose father had him baptized at the age of six. He was thus able to take the Christian oath before entering Parliament. Disraeli was void of religious convictions, calling himself "the blank page between the Old and New Testaments" yet to friend and foe alike he remained a Jew, albeit a Christian Jew.

The composer Wagner railed against such Jewish influence in German life, and pioneered his own anti-Jewish hatred, which would emerge in his writings and music, and be a source for the anti-Semitic propaganda of Hitler and the Nazis a century later. Jewish intellectuals such as Heinrich Heine, Karl Marx, and Emma Lazarus in the USA ("give me your poor"), made contributions in wider society that would shape political, academic, and artistic life. But negative reactions arose. Anti-Semitism continued, and in some places, such as Russia and Poland, became worse. Between 1890 and 1905 pogroms broke out in Russia, as part of the Czar's policy of "russification": either the Jews left Russia, served in the army for twenty-five years, or were baptized. This led to millions leaving the "Pale of Settlement," an area of Russia, Poland, and Eastern Europe, fleeing the pogroms and going either to Israel, the United States, or other parts of Europe.

In 1897 Theodore Herzl, a Jewish journalist from Vienna, gathered the first Zionist Congress. He had seen the unfair trial of Alfred Dreyfus in France, and proposed the resettlement of the Jews in Palestine as the best way to solve the problem of anti-Semitism in Europe. His book *The Jewish State* became the blueprint for what would become the Zionist programme, a diplomatic initiative to gain support for the re-establishment of the State of Israel. In 1917 Lord Balfour, Prime Minister of the United Kingdom, wrote to Lord Rothschild and issued the declaration:

> His Majesty's Government view with favour the establishment in Palestine of a national home for the Jewish people, and will use their best endeavours to facilitate the achievement of the object, it being clearly understood that nothing shall be done which may prejudice the civil and religious rights of existing non-Jewish communities in Palestine, or the rights and political status enjoyed by Jews in any other country.[4]

The Russian Jewish exodus helped to settle Palestine, which was barely populated and needed its swampland draining and the land made farmable. The waves of Aliyah ("going up") produced new cities such as Tel Aviv, Petach Tikvah, and Rishon-le-Tzion. Until the First World War, Jews lived alongside the Arabs in Palestine relatively peacefully, but after the war, when Palestine was under the British Mandate, relations between Jews, Arabs, and the British became increasingly violent, and no international solution was able to solve the problem.

The period between the two World Wars saw the growth of the Jewish presence in Palestine, and the growth of the Jewish population worldwide to approximately 14 million. But tragedy was on the horizon, and when Hitler came to power in Germany in 1933 he not only unleashed the Second World War but put into

4. Schneer, *The Balfour Declaration*, 5.

action his plan to wipe out the Jewish people from the face of the planet: the "Final Solution" to the Jewish question.

The Holocaust

The Hirschland family, taken circa 1850–60. Personal collection.
Left to right: Moses (my great-great-grandfather), Simon,
Abraham, Salomon, Levi.

My family come from Germany—the Hirschlands from Essen. Over the centuries they lived and worked in Germany, in prosperous trades and professions: doctors, lawyers, bankers, etc.[5] The family tree can be traced back to 1475. My cousin Kester says that,

5. Kester, "Hirschland Family," http://www.thekesters.net/Genealogy/

In the 1700's [sic] the majority of the population of Europe was engaged in farming. Jews, however, were forbidden from owning land, so they rarely were farmers. Instead, many of them were itinerant traders, walking farm-to-farm, village-to-village, buying and selling things, often dealing in cattle. By the early 1800's [sic] many of them would sell things from their homes; later they would open shops. Simon Hirschland in Essen was one of these small shopkeepers. Things he sold included wool, meat, pelts, nails, copper, lead, and cattle. Oftentimes, his customers were unable to immediately pay him for merchandise, so he would sell on credit. This lending part of the business grew, and in 1841 Simon started a small banking business, the Simon Hirschland Bank. The bank was very successful, becoming, under the direction of Simon's son Isaac, one of the largest banks in Germany. It was instrumental in financing many of the industries of the Ruhrgebiet, the industrial heartland of Germany centered around Essen. They were bankers to the Krupps, also based in Essen, Germany's largest armaments manufacturer, and in the late 1800s the largest industrial company in the world.[6]

But the fate of the Hirschlands was to change. I was sitting in the Leo Baeck Institute of Jewish history in New York when I came across a folder of some twenty pages of names of my family, and their locations in Germany and around the world, that had the Gestapo stamp on it. My German is pretty poor, but I realized that this was a list compiled just before World War II showing where the more than 1,000 family members were living. Was this so they could be tracked down, arrested, or possibly—as the Hirschland Bank was the last to be taken over by the Nazis, as it was bringing money into Germany to build up the war effort—to protect them?

Whatever the answer, the situation was clear. Those who left Germany, coming to the UK, USA, and Israel, survived. Those who stayed perished. The synagogue in Essen (now a Jewish museum and cultural center) has a memorial book of those who lost their

Hirschland.html.

6. Ibid.

lives in the Shoah (Holocaust). There are many Hirschlands in it, their names and those who were deported being visible to all. One of my cousins came over on the *kindertransport* and wrote *A Boy in Your Situation.*[7]

The fate of the Hirschlands was magnified by the millions. Over the ten year period from 1935–45 some 6 million Jews, and 5 million others (gypsies, Slavs, Poles, homosexuals, mentally ill people, communists, conscientious objectors) would be put to death in the gas chambers and work camps set up by the Nazis. The coordinated effort of identifying, rounding up, and transporting to the concentration camps took major human resources and organization. For propaganda to persuade the German people, the Austrians, French, Romanians, Poles, and Italians, the sermons of Luther were reprinted and distributed, and we shall examine this further in the following chapter.

The Reestablishment of the State of Israel to the Present Day

Out of the darkness of the Shoah came the light of a new dawn. Hundreds of thousands of displaced survivors, refugees from their homes that had been destroyed in Europe, made their way to Israel. There, joined by immigrants from the Middle East, North Africa, and around the world, the small country of Israel welcomed them. The Law of Return stated that anyone with one Jewish grandparent could become a citizen of the new State of Israel, and over the decades of the twentieth century Israel welcomed immigrants from the former Soviet Union (1 million), Ethiopia, Iran, Iraq, etc.

Today Israel is a busy, bustling country. Half its 6-million population is under the age of thirty-five. In addition to Hebrew and Arabic (23 percent of its inhabitants), Russian, French, Spanish, and many other languages are spoken. It is a curious blend of the old, of tradition and religion stretching back thousands of years, and the new, with the latest in start-up companies,

7. Hannam, *A Boy in Your Situation,* 25.

information technology, media and advertising, and the most so-phisticated weapon systems and military hardware. Defence plays a major part in the life of the country, with all eighteen-to-twenty-year-olds serving in the army, and a major war every ten years or so. Following wars in 1948, 1956, 1967, 1974, 1982, and right up to the war in Gaza in 2014, everyone knows the reality of the air-raid sirens, the bomb shelters, and serving in the military reserves.

For Jewish people around the world, the horrors of the Ho-locaust have receded, but many are still worried at the increase of anti-Semitism worldwide. The attacks on Jewish people in a kosher supermarket in Paris in January 2015 highlighted the sense of fear and danger. The ongoing conflict in Israel/Palestine seems intrac-table, long-term, and violent, and there is little room for negotiation, conflict resolution, and not much sign of a just settlement in sight.

Jewish Population

There are now some 16 million Jewish people worldwide, with about half living in Israel. The Diaspora communities are aging and declining, with a few exceptions, such as in Brazil and Germany. The State of Israel is home to a vibrant and growing community, with more than half under the age of thirty-five. Immigration to Israel continues, with about 10,000 a year arriving, either to escape anti-Semitism, or to fulfill the Zionist vision of a new life in a new land, a Jewish homeland.

The Orthodox and Ultra-Orthodox communities are grow-ing faster than the secular, with many having an average of eight children or more.

The Jewish community in the UK, in which I grew up, peaked at 410,000 in the 1960s due to immigration after World War II and the baby boom in the 1950s and 1960s. Today the official figure stands at 350,000 (those associated with synagogues), but the un-official figure is about double that. Jewish people still make up less than 1 percent of the UK population, but have made significant contributions to the life, culture, and politics of the country, with Jews visible in every aspect of its life.

The situation in Germany is very different, and marks a stark and cold contrast, which I feel whenever I visit my family's ancestral origins. In the nineteenth and early twentieth centuries Jewish people were greatly involved in the life of the country, and prominent in all aspects of the culture and society of the day. But the tide of integration and assimilation was reversed by Hitler's policies of discrimination. The Nuremberg Laws passed in 1935 prevented Jews from working in the civil service, medicine, education, law, and other professions (all but the most menial of professions), and prevented marriage with non-Jews.[8] Arrest, deportation, forced labor, and death were the fate of 210,000 of the 240,000 in Germany, 3 million in Poland, and other countries.[9]

The following figures from Lucy Dawidowicz show the annihilation of the Jewish population of Europe by (pre-war) country:

8. https://en.wikipedia.org/wiki/Nuremberg_Laws.

9. https://en.wikipedia.org/wiki/The_Holocaust#Jewish.

Country	Pre-Final Solution Jewish Population	Jewish Population Killed in Final Solution	Percent Killed
Poland	3,300,000	3,000,000	90%
Baltic Countries	253,000	228,000	90%
Germany/Austria	240,000	210,000	88%
Protectorate	90,000	80,000	89%
Slovakia	90,000	75,000	83%
Greece	70,000	54,000	77%
The Netherlands	140,000	105,000	75%
Hungary	650,000	450,000	70%
White Russia	375,000	245,000	65%
Ukraine	1,500,000	900,000	60%
Belgium	65,000	40,000	60%
Yugoslavia	43,000	26,000	60%
Romania	600,000	300,000	50%
Norway	1,800	900	50%
France	350,000	90,000	26%
Bulgaria	64,000	14,000	22%
Italy	40,000	8,000	20%
Luxembourg	5,000	1,000	20%
Russia	975,000	107,000	11%
Denmark	8,000	—	—
Finland	2,000	—	—
Total	8,861,800	5,933,900	67%

History of the Jews during World War II

Today, Germany is home to some 200,000[10] Jewish immigrants from the former Soviet Union countries, and about 10,000 Israelis. They have been welcomed back into the country and given generous opportunities to settle, study, and raise their families. Some

10. http://forward.com/news/4029/germany-is-moving-to-end-mass -immigration-of-jews/

of those who came from Russia are now believers in Jesus, and there are twenty-five Messianic Jewish groups in Germany, mainly composed of Russian-speaking Jewish believers in Jesus and their families, the next generation of whom are German-speaking and integrating quickly into German society.

In 1991, the Jewish population of Germany stood at 31,000 German-speaking Jews. Today, the population stands at 230,000 Jewish people, of which 200,000 are Russian-speaking Jewish immigrants who have moved to Germany, mostly in the last twenty years. This has made Germany one of the largest Jewish population centers in Europe.

Messianic Jews in History and Today

Many Jewish people accepted Jesus as the Messiah and when, after his crucifixion, the belief in his rising from the dead spread amongst them, they became one of the many sects within the Jewish community of their day. Over the following few decades, with war with the Romans resulting in the destruction of the temple (70 CE) and the banishing of Jews from Jerusalem, the small group of Jewish followers of Jesus, known as "Nazarenes," "followers of the Way," and "Ebionites" ("the poor ones," either in terms of doctrine or material wealth) were on the margins of both Jewish society and the increasingly non-Jewish church.

Initially there were accepted by the church fathers—Jerome, Justin Martyr, Epiphanius—but as Judaism and Christianity went their separate ways in the fourth century, it became increasingly unacceptable to both ecclesiastical and rabbinic authorities to grant the legitimacy of Jewish expressions of faith in Christ. Excluded from the synagogue for their belief in the Trinity and divinity of Christ, and they were anathematized by the church for continued practice of Jewish customs and were constantly suspected of legalism and adoptionist Christology (which said that Jesus was not fully God in the same way that the Father is God).

When in 132–25 CE Bar Kokhba led a revolt against the Romans, he was proclaimed the Messiah by a prominent rabbi,

Akiva, and even had coins minted with his messianic claims to be the Davidic King. But his revolt failed, his followers committed suicide rather than be captured on top of the fortress of Mount Masada near the Dead Sea, and the Jewish revolt was in tatters. The Jesus-believing Jews had previously left the city and were holed up in nearby Pella, across the river Jordan. But they remained a small, isolated group, on the margins of both the Jewish people and the growing Christian church. Over the next few centuries, whilst they remained in communities scattered across the Roman Empire and further to the east as far as China, India, and Persia, they were caught between the two groups.

The rabbinic tradition grew so that rabbis became the guardians of the Jewish community, for its beliefs, practices, and membership. If you believed in Jesus as Messiah, perhaps that could be tolerated, but if you accepted him as Son of God, God in human form, that was beyond acceptance. Strict Jewish monotheism said that God could have no physical form and no human should be elevated to the status of the divine, as that constituted idolatry.

So Jewish believers in Jesus were caught in the crossfire and conflicts between Christians and Jews, and continue to be part of the troubled relationship between the two communities. When the Emperor Constantine embraced Christianity and it became the official religion of the Roman Empire, a series of councils (Nicea, Chalcedon, etc.) not only consolidated the religion, but passed a series of laws against the continued observance of Jewish festivals and practices, of Christians marrying or doing business with Jews, and of Jews owning Christian slaves.

Some Hebrew Christians, as they came to be called, helped to translate the Scriptures from Hebrew into Latin and the languages of Europe. Others, relying on what appeared to be the offer of generous royal protection, quickly discovered that they were now excluded from their homes and families, had lost their property and possessions, and could not easily find work. In the Middle Ages converts' homes (*Domus Conversorum*) were set up to provide protection to those who became Christians, often under duress and forced to listen to sermons from visiting friars or take part in disputations which were held under threat.

The medieval period, with its Crusades, Spanish Inquisition, and blood libels, made relations between Jews and Christians strained. The Reformation and Renaissance in Europe allowed greater freedom and interaction between the two groups, and Jewish believers in Jesus helped in Bible translation, the printing of Hebrew books, and the development of Protestant theology. Others followed, and in the nineteenth and twentieth centuries large numbers of Jewish people became Christians, some for commercial reasons, but others out of genuine conviction.

Today there are more than 100,000 Jewish believers in Jesus who identify themselves as Hebrew Christians, Jewish Christians, Messianic Jews, or some other term that shows they are *both* Jewish *and* believe in Jesus. Organizations like the International Messianic Jewish Alliance, with national alliances worldwide, the Helsinki Consultation on Jewish Continuity in the Body of Christ, and groups like Jews for Jesus, have brought together a large number of Messianic Jews (my preferred term) in congregations, fellowships, networks, and cooperative projects.

The medieval period is known for the persecution of the Jewish people by the church (both Roman Catholics and Protestants, such as Luther) through the Crusades, Inquisition, forced conversions, and the expulsion of Jews from many European countries. Medieval anti-Semitism perpetrated images of the Jews as the poisoners of wells (causing the Black Death), depicting them suckling pigs, desecrating the Host, and kidnapping Christian children to use their blood in Passover sacrifices. Forced to listen to sermons and engage in disputations, which if won by the Jewish side led to further penalties, the medieval Jewish community lived under constant threat of confiscation of their homes and possessions, and danger to their lives.

However, as I have already said, many became Christians, some out of political expediency and for survival, others out of genuine conviction. Some, such as Theresa D'Avila, Paul of Burgos, Nicholas de Lyra, and Emmanuel Tremellius, made great contributions to faith and theology in the church. Throughout this period and into the Reformation and Renaissance, Jewish Christians helped with the development of Bible translation and Hebrew studies in the church, and enlarged European understanding of Jews and Judaism.

In 1809, Joseph Samuel Christian Frederick Frey, from Posen, Hungary, encouraged the formation of the London Society for the Promotion of Christianity among the Jews, which later became the Church's Ministry among the Jewish People (CMJ). In 1813, Frey founded the Beni Abraham, a community of Jewish Christians that met under the auspices of Anglicans. Encouraged by CMJ and other Jewish missions, the growing number of Hebrew Christians, as they called themselves, formed their own Prayer Union (1866), British (1888) and International Alliances (1925), and developed their own liturgies and Hebrew Christian churches in Europe, Palestine, and the USA.[11]

By the end of the nineteenth century it was estimated on the basis of baptismal statistics that over a million Jewish people had become Christians, many for reasons of assimilation and emancipation from the ghettos into European society with access to commerce, education, and secular society. Nevertheless, a recognizable number—such as Alfred Edersheim, Adolph Saphir, Augustus Neander, and Bishop Samuel Shereshewsky—wished to retain aspects of their Jewish identity alongside genuine faith in Christ. They were a blessing to the church and a testimony to their people.[12]

After the Second World War, the Holocaust, and the establishment of the State of Israel, Jewish believers in Jesus from a new generation were concerned to rediscover their ethnic roots and express their faith from a Jewish perspective. In the wake of the Jesus movement of the 1970s, "Jews for Jesus" moved from a slogan used on the streets of San Francisco to a global organization. At the same time, the Messianic Jewish Alliance of America encouraged the establishment of Messianic congregations and synagogues. In Israel a new generation of native-born Israelis (*sabras*) were

11. Darby, *The Emergence of the Hebrew Christian Movement,* 182.

12. Schonfield, *The History of Jewish Christianity,* 10.

finding the Messiah and starting Hebrew-speaking congregations. By the end of the twentieth century an international network of Messianic groups had come into existence with denominational, theological, and cultural distinctives, yet united with the gentile church and with one another by their common in belief in Yeshua.

Messianic Judaism can be defined as a Jewish form of Christianity and a Christian form of Judaism—a cultural, religious, and theological expression adopted in recent years by an increasing number of Jewish people worldwide who believe in Yeshua (as Jews often prefer to call him) as the promised Messiah. Messianic Judaism finds its expression in Messianic congregations and synagogues and in the individual lifestyle of Messianic Jews who combine Jewish identity with belief in Jesus.

Contemporary Expression

Today there are some 150,000 Jewish believers in Jesus worldwide, according to conservative estimates. More than 100,000 are in the US, approximately 15,000 in Israel, and the remainder are found throughout the 16 million Jewish population worldwide. There are over 300 Messianic groups in the US and over 120 in Israel. While they are not uniform in their beliefs and expression, the majority adhere to orthodox Christian beliefs on the uniqueness and deity of Christ, the Trinity, the authority of Scripture, and so forth, while expressing these beliefs in a Jewish cultural and religious context that affirms the continuing election of Israel, understood as the Jewish people, and the ongoing purposes of God for His people.[13]

Messianic Jews to varying degrees observe the Sabbath, keep kosher food laws, circumcise their sons, and celebrate the Jewish festivals, seeing Jesus and the church in Acts as their models and examples. They celebrate Passover, showing how Yeshua came as the Passover lamb, and practice baptism as linked to the Jewish

13. There are no accurate statistics for the numbers of self-identifying Jewish believers in Jesus, and the term "Messianic Jew/Judaism" continues to be subject to negotiation and boundary-processing. For a recent discussion see Harvey, *The Conversion of Non-Jews to Messianic Judaism*, 1–31.

mikveh or "ritual bath." They worship with their own liturgies based on the synagogue service with readings from the Torah and the New Testament. Pointing to Paul's teaching in Romans 9–11 and his practice on missionary journeys, their hermeneutic of Scripture repudiates traditional Christian anti-Judaism ("the Jews killed Christ") and supersessionism (the church has replaced Israel and become the "new Israel"), arguing for forms of Torah observance that testify to the presence of the believing remnant in the midst of unbelieving Israel as a witness to the Messiah.

CHAPTER 3

Luther's Lies about the Jews

What is Anti-Semitism?

W<small>E ARE GOING TO</small> be discussing Luther's attitudes to Jews and Judaism—how he understood the Jewish people—and his views on the Jewish religion, both in his own day and at the time of Jesus. Scholars often distinguish between theological anti-Judaism, and political or social anti-Semitism.[1] Here is one statement by a meeting of Lutherans distinguishing between the two:

> We use "anti-Judaism" to name specifically theological formulations that denigrate Jews and their faith. Looking at the roots of anti-Judaism in Christian theology, it can be understood as a phenomenon of the separation of the church from Judaism. Later on, other motives (social, political, economic, racist) became dominant and led to exclusion and persecution of Jews through centuries. In "antisemitism," we refer to a broader reality: the hatred of and hostility toward Jews, in reality and in rhetoric, that denies them legitimacy among the peoples of the world. This hatred and hostility is to be understood within the larger issues of racism and is countered by

1. The term anti-Semitism was coined by Wilhelm Marr in 1879. It can be written as "antisemitism," "anti-Semitism," or "anti-semitism." It is an inaccurate term to describe opposition to Jewish people alone, as the Semites, descendants of Noah's son Shem (Gen 5:32), include several other nations as well as the Hebrews (descendants of Eber, Gen 10:31), including the Arabs, Elamites, Assyrians, and Arameans.

the affirmation of human rights that has been part of our heritage for more than 50 years.[2]

As we will see, Luther did not distinguish much between the Jewish people and their religion, or the Jewish people at the time of Jesus and in his own day. He also did not really distinguish between the majority of Jews who did not believe in Jesus, and the very small minority who did.

For Luther, as we shall see, the more modern distinction between anti-Judaism and anti-Semitism did not really matter. For my family, most of whom do not believe in Jesus, and myself, a Messianic Jew, it does not make much difference either. Luther's lies led to the Nazi extermination project, which did not distinguish between Jewish believers in Jesus and others, but included anyone of Jewish descent, regardless of their religious views.[3]

Is the New Testament Anti-Semitic?

I remember as a young disciple the first sermon I heard that told me that the Jews were "stiff-necked." Bristling with anger at the use of such an offensive stereotype I went up to the preacher after the service, stuck my neck out at him, and demanded he tell me how many stiff-necked Jews he knew! He was appropriately apologetic, and we have remained good friends to this day, some forty years later. But as a Jewish believer in Jesus I have remained very sensitive to anti-Jewish stereotypes, whether they are a product of religious and theological anti-Judaism, or racial and ethnic anti-Semitism.

Some scholars see the writings of the New Testament as anti-Semitic. After all, in John's Gospel, doesn't Jesus call the Jews "children of the devil"? Doesn't he tell them that they will perish because they have not believed in him? In Matthew's Gospel

2. See my blog: "13 September 2001. Lutherans Reflect on Antisemitism and Anti-Judaism #otdimjh."

3. Some scholars also talk about "non-rational antijudaism" and "irrational" anti-Semitism—but again, according to Langmuir, this is a step too far, and is not necessary or helpful. See Langmuir, "From Anti-Judaism to Anti-semitism." For extended discussion see also Falk, *Anti-semitism*.

Jesus has strong condemnation of the Pharisees, saying they are hypocrites, white-washed tombs, who will have the kingdom taken from them and given to others because they have taken the vineyard owner's son and murdered him. There is a strong critical element against Jews and Judaism throughout the New Testament. Paul's opponents are Jews or Jewish Christians who want to persuade all believers in Jesus from the nations (gentiles) to be circumcised and keep the law of Moses, and Paul often has harsh words for them. The wrath of God has come upon them for preventing Paul from preaching to the gentiles (1 Thess 2:16). The book of Revelation describes a "synagogue of Satan," which commentators often understand to be the rival Jewish community in Philadelphia (Rev 3:9).

Particularly when it comes to the Pharisees, it seems that they are a bad lot. Jesus's "woes to the Pharisees" in Luke 11:37–54 and Matthew 23:1–39 are full of condemnations of their legalism, hypocrisy, and heartlessness. What are we to make of his condemnation of the Jewish religious leaders of his day? Did Jesus see the Jewish groups of his day in such a negative way, or are we overhearing a family quarrel, with admittedly heated exchanges typical of a Jewish family argument, and then taking this out of context as a blanket condemnation of all his opponents were and stood for?

Traditionally Christians have interpreted these passages to show the spiritual bankruptcy and hypocrisy of the Jewish establishment leaders, and the inferiority of Judaism. But if we understand Jesus' own practices, and his connections with the Jewish life of his day, is it so clear? What many Christians fail to notice, as Luther himself was to do, was that Jesus' own teaching, life, and practice was very close to that of the Jewish religious groups of his day, especially of the Pharisees, the forerunners of the rabbinic Judaism that would emerge after the destruction of the temple in 70 CE and the war with Rome in 132–35 CE. In fact, Jesus' teaching is seeped with the wisdom and doctrines of the Pharisees, and echoes many of their finest sayings. Only later, in the fourth and fifth centuries CE, when Judaism and Christianity became two separate religions, was it possible to set Christianity against Judaism. Only with the later church fathers, such as Chrysostom, did the condemnation of Jewish religious leaders become transformed into a condemnation of Jewish people and Jewish faith.

In popular usage and Christian tradition the term "Pharisee" implies legalism, hypocrisy, obstinate refusal to believe in Jesus, and opposition to him, because of centuries of misunderstanding of the Pharisees and Jesus' relationship to them. But who were the Pharisees, and what did they really teach and practice? We find the evidence for and information about them not just in the New Testament, but also in Josephus and the rabbinic tradition. When we compare this with the portrayals of them in the New Testament, such as the seven "woes" of Matthew 23:1–36, we realize that this is an internal family debate taking place *within* the Jewish community, not an "outsider" attacking "foreigners" or those who are different to him. The traditional negative views of the Pharisees need to be re-appraised in the light of modern scholarship and a post-supersessionist understanding of the relationship between Christianity and Judaism, reclaiming the Pharisees as a vital and essential part of the Jesus-believing Jewish movement that became the church of today. Unfortunately, Luther lived at a time where such new studies were unavailable, and such an approach would have gone against one of his main aims, of proving the rabbis were wrong in not accepting Jesus as their Messiah. Luther set out to justify his own faith and position by mercilessly attacking that of his opponents, chief among whom were the Jewish people who still, after 1,500 years, refused to accept the Christian faith.

So we must be careful to understand rightly such difficult passages in their context. The prophets of ancient Israel were no less condemning of their own people. Jeremiah rails against Israel as a faithless woman who has abandoned her husband. Hosea speaks of the adultery of Israel. Isaiah despises the hypocrisy of false worship offered by the Israelites in the temple. Rather than condemning the Jews as outsiders, wishing them to be destroyed, these strong and vivid Jewish expressions, where the outpouring of emotion is accompanied by hyperbole (a rhetorical exaggeration), should be seen as the prophets' very strong commitment to their people, and their desperate desire to see Israel repent and return to God. Nowhere in the Old Testament does God give up on his people, but is always longing to renew his covenant commitment and relationship to them.

Likewise, Jesus and the writers of the New Testament should be seen as speaking *within* and *to* their own people, not as condemning them from outside. Whilst they speak strongly, and later Christians saw this as a denunciation of the Jewish people and the religion of Judaism, which meant that God had finished with them and transferred his choice of the people of God onto the church, in fact, it is because of God's mercy, justice, and passionate and possessive love of Israel that he cannot bear to see them go away from him, but also cannot and will not abandon them. For every passage that speaks of Israel's faithlessness, which will lead to punishment and exile because they have abandoned the covenant, there are even more passages that speak of God's faithfulness to his covenant and to his people, even when they are faithless.

So too the condemnations and judgments of Jesus, Paul, and other New Testament writers must be seen against the background of the ongoing election of Israel and God's faithfulness to his covenant, and his ultimate purpose to regather, restore, and renew his people Israel, as a sign of his character of faithfulness, to show all nations his saving power.

What is the History of Jewish-Christian Relations up to and beyond Luther?

Throughout the history of the church, such a position has been turned on its head, as the majority of the early church fathers argued the opposite, that God had *finished* with the Jewish people, because the church (made up mostly of the nations) had become the *new* Israel, the *true* Israel. And furthermore, the old Israel, the Jewish people, were condemned to wander the earth, without a king or a home, as "reluctant witnesses" of their involvement in the crucifixion of Christ.[4]

This reading of the Bible accounts by the early church fathers is known as "supersessionism" (with one group "sitting in the place of another, superseding them") or "replacement theology." While its early forms were developed by Justin Martyr and Irenaeus, the classic expression was given by Chrysostom and Augustine. Luther, as an Augustinian monk, inherited the views of Augustine on Jews and Judaism, and did not add to them, except in the degree to which he expressed them, and in the consequences his conveying them would have.

According to this view, God's choice of Israel (the Jewish people) to be his covenant people had been changed. Now the church is the new Israel, the Jews have forfeited their land (Israel), their holy city (Jerusalem), and their holy temple, because they rejected the Son of God. He has now fulfilled all the Old Testament promises, and the symbols of the land, city, temple, and people of Israel have now been transferred to and fulfilled in the church, the people of God.

While there is some truth in this, and Reformers like Luther were quick to show how the Old Testament promises were now to be applied to all Christians who made up the church in the new covenant, there is a dark side to this teaching, which has led to Jews being denigrated, singled out, persecuted, and seen as the enemies of God and of Christianity. It was the duty of Christians to avoid them, not have dealings with them, and see them as the "reluctant witnesses" (Augustine) God had preserved to wander the face of the earth, like disobedient, murderous Cain, until the second coming when Jesus would, at the end of days, cause the Jews to repent and believe, though Luther himself questioned whether this was possible.

4. Fredricksen, *Augustine and the Jews,* shows how Augustine developed his understanding of the Jews to show that God had preserved them (and so they should not be eliminated) specifically to demonstrate by their rejection of Jesus the truth of Christianity and the failure of Judaism. Luther, as an Augustinian novice, was taught this view from his early days as a monk, and added to it with vigor.

By the time of Luther the Christian tradition had not only condemned the Jewish people for killing Christ, seeing their exile from the land of Israel as a just punishment, but had enacted legislation to oppress them and limit their freedom. In the early centuries of the Christian church both Jews and Christians were persecuted by the Roman pagan emperors and they were often united. Many Jews were Christians, and Christianity was still conscious of its continuity with the Jewish people. Jewish slaves built the Colosseum in Rome where Christians, many of them also Jewish, were fed to the lions as martyrs.

But when the Emperor Constantine adopted Christianity as the official religion of the Roman Empire and convened church councils at Nicaea (325 CE) and Chalcedon (451 CE), at the same time as defining a unified set of doctrines and creeds to unite Christians throughout the empire, a set of anti-Jewish laws was passed to prevent Christians observing Jewish traditions and practices, marrying Jewish spouses, condemning such things as heretical, and isolating Jews from wider Roman and Christian society.

The Jews and Christians could barely be distinguished at the start of Christianity. All believers in Jesus, whether from Israel or the nations (Jew or gentile), worshipped together, as synagogues and churches had not become two separate institutions, let alone buildings. Both Jews and Christians were persecuted by the Romans, and expelled from Rome in 49 CE by the Emperor Claudius. Nero persecuted the Christians in 64 CE, blaming them for the great fire. In 66–70 CE the Jewish revolt against Rome led to the siege of Jerusalem and destruction of the temple in 70 CE by the Emperor Titus. According to Eusebius' *Church History*, the Jewish Christians were warned to leave Jerusalem before its destruction, and fled across the River Jordan to settle in Pella, where they continued for several centuries.

By the time the Jewish revolt was put down and the remaining rebels under Bar Kocheba had committed suicide on Mount Masada in 135 CE, the Christian church had become majority non-Jewish, and had established itself in the Diaspora.

The church fathers began the process of translating and authorizing the texts of the Old and New Testaments, entering into dialogue and debate with Jews, and trying to live under Roman rule and the polytheistic Roman society, which worshipped idols and the emperor.

The early church grew apart from Jews and Judaism, although it could not help having a love-hate relationship with all things Jewish. What Christians called the "Old Testament" was originally written in Hebrew,[5] Jesus celebrated the Sabbath and the Jewish festivals, and Christian morality was based on the law of the Old Testament, especially the Ten Commandments.

Marcion, a Christian heretic of the second century (140–85), was excommunicated for teaching that the God of the Old Testament was a God of anger and judgment, and not the same as the God of love and mercy in the New. He wanted to get rid of the Old Testament, and large parts of the New. But the church fathers, such as Justin Martyr (100–165) and Origen (185–253), preferred to retain and spiritualize the Old Testament, seeing in the history of Israel, her battles, enemies, and conquering of the promised land an allegorical and symbolic meaning about the inner spiritual life of the believer and the church, rather than having any national or political significance.

In 190, Pope Victor I excommunicated any churches or Christians who observed Easter on the Jewish date for Passover, the 14th Nisan, thus severing the link between Judaism and Christianity further. Edicts were passed preventing Christians from celebrating Jewish festivals, marrying Jewish spouses, attending synagogues or Jewish homes, all with the aim of separating the two faith communities. The fact that such laws were repeatedly passed and re-affirmed over the centuries is a strong indicator that at the level of ordinary people they were largely ignored. In fact, many Jewish Christians continued to be part of both communities, and Agobard of Lyons (779–840) is quite jealous that Christians enjoy the sermons of the rabbis in the synagogue and prefer to go there rather than the church: "It even reaches the point when

5. I prefer the term Hebrew Bible to Old Testament.

naive Christians say that the Jews preach to them better than our priests."[6]

In 380 Christianity became the official religion of the Roman Empire, and the creeds and councils of Nicaea and Chalcedon unified Christian beliefs across the empire, and passed further decrees anathematizing (condemning and banning) Jews, Judaism, and Jewish practices within the church.

The distancing was mutual. On the Jewish side, around the year 400 the Jerusalem Talmud was compiled, and in 500 the larger Babylonian Talmud. The Jewish synagogue liturgy now included a curse, the *Birkat Haminim* ("'blessing' on heretics"). It affirms the strict monotheism as defined by the rabbis, which meant that no Jew could believe in the possibility of the Trinity, the plural unity of God, or the idea of the incarnation, that God could or would take on physical human form.

By the time of the First Crusade (1095) relations between Jews and Christians were under suspicion. Jews were permitted

---

6. In his writings "On the Insolence of the Jews" (written to Louis the Pious in 826), Agobard calls the Jews "children of the devil": "Most pious lord, I have mentioned only a few out of the many things concerning the faithlessness of the Jews, our admonition, and the wounding of Christianity that is occurring through the supporters of the Jews, since I do not know whether [this news] can even come to your attention. Nonetheless, it is absolutely necessary that your pious solicitude know how the Christian faith is being harmed by the Jews in certain ways. For when they lie to simple Christians and boast that they are dear to you because of the patriarchs; that they enter and leave your sight with honor; that most excellent people desire their prayers and blessings and confess that they wished they had the same author of the law as the Jews; when they say that your counselors are aroused against us for their sake, because we forbid Christians from drinking their wine; when, in trying to claim this, they boast that they have received from Christians many, many pounds of silver from the sale of wine and cannot find out, after running through the canons, why Christians should abstain from their food and drink; when they produce commands signed with golden seals in your name and containing words which, in our opinion, are not true; when they show people women's clothes as if they were sent to their wives by your kinsmen or matrons of the palaces; when they expound upon the glory of their forefathers; when they are permitted, contrary to the law, to build new synagogues—[when all this occurs] it even reaches the point when naive Christians say that the Jews preach to them better than our priests."

to lend money (*usury*), but had no security should the king or his nobles refuse payment. Throughout the medieval period the Roman Catholic Church passed a series of laws ("Decretales") limiting Jewish people in their trades and professions, their rights to travel and settle, their employment of Christian servants, who they were permitted to marry, and all other freedoms. They were forced to wear distinctive clothes, such as a pointed hat, or to wear a six-pointed Jewish star on their garments. They were locked up at night in restricted areas known as *ghettos* and not allowed safe passage outside without paying large sums of money for papal protection. They were forced to listen to sermons and disputations trying to convert them to Christianity, and houses for converts offered them financial inducements to do so.

Disputations between Jews and Christians never took place on a level playing field. If the Jews won, they were banished or put to death. If they lost, they were forcibly converted. The monastic orders, the Benedictines and the Franciscans, took a particular interest in developing arguments with which to confront the Jewish leaders to show that Jesus was the Messiah and that the Jews should stop resisting him. The most well-known manual for arguing with Jews and Muslims, the *Dagger of Faith* (*Pugio Fidei*), portrayed both Jews and Muslims submitting to the superior knowledge and arguments of Christian preachers. Out of the dunghill of Jewish tradition Christians were taught to find "pearls" of wisdom, showing the truth of the Christian faith was even present in Jewish tradition, if you knew how to look.

The frontispiece of the *Pugio Fidei* (*Dagger of Faith*) showing both Muslim and Jew beneath the dagger of the Christian arguments[7]

7. Public domain—Lithography and title page of *Pugio fidei* (Edition

In such a difficult context, the Crusades from the eleventh to the fifteenth centuries were particularly nasty examples of outbreaks of violence against the Jewish people. Popes, princes, ordinary people, pardoned criminals, and even children would take up arms and march through Europe on their way to free the Holy Land from the Turks. When they passed through Jewish towns and villages, vandalism, looting, rape, and massacres were common.

Two further events cast a shadow of fear over the lives of the Jewish people in the Middle Ages. They were blamed for poisoning wells, and the Black Death (1348). Where modern health regulations and medical treatment were not available, Jewish doctors were often more advanced in their treatment of disease than non-Jewish physicians. But they were still blamed when sickness arose, and were accused of poisoning their patients. The Black Death led to massacres of Jews throughout Europe; people reasoned that as there was no other explanation, the Jews must be to blame for the plague that decimated the European population. Nine hundred Jews were burnt at the stake in Strasbourg on Valentine's Day 1349 for their alleged part in the Black Death, a particularly gruesome occurrence.[8]

Notable instances of persecution include the pogroms that preceded the First Crusade in 1096, the expulsion of the Jewish community from England in 1290, massacres of Spanish Jews in 1391, the persecutions of the Spanish Inquisition (1480 onwards), and the expulsions from Spain and Portugal in 1492 and 1497.

Such was the context in which Luther would come to prominence. He grew up believing the lies about the Jews, and inherited from Augustine and the early church fathers the belief that the Jews deserved such punishments, being condemned to wander the earth without a homeland as a punishment for their rejection of Jesus Christ and as "reluctant witnesses" to the truth they had rejected.

Leipzig, 1687) https://it.wikipedia.org/wiki/Raimondo_Mart%C3%AD#/media/File:Pugio.png.

8. Harvey, "14 February 1349."

After Luther's time and up to the present, the persecution continued with the Cossack massacres in Ukraine of 1648–57, various pogroms in Imperial Russia between 1821 and 1906, the 1894–1906 Dreyfus affair in France, the Holocaust in German-occupied Europe (1939–45), official Soviet anti-Jewish policies, and Arab and Muslim involvement in the Jewish exodus from Arab and Muslim countries.

CHAPTER 4

What Did Luther Say about the Jews?

As a Jew, Luther's writings on Jews and Judaism make me angry, sad, and afraid. How could a man of such learning, with such genius, great insight into the key truths of the gospel, who loved the Bible as God's word, and who had such a profound experience of the grace of God, be so vitriolic and intemperate in his hostility to the Jewish people? I remember my first reading of his work *On the Jews and Their Lies* and could not believe it. But what he wrote and said about the Jews is the subject we must now focus on. May God give us mercy and keep us from such prejudice and hatred towards others!

Several scholars try to excuse or explain Luther's anti-Judaism in a variety of ways. He was a man of his time, and it was an age seeped in prejudice against the Jews. Luther began with a good attitude towards the Jewish people, hoping they would convert and join him in his struggle against the papacy. He was an angry, embittered, and unwell man when he wrote his diatribes against the Jews, and these were against his better judgment. Some have argued unconvincingly that Luther repented of his anti-Semitic views on his deathbed. His colleagues and contemporaries disassociated themselves from his intemperate remarks, as have most Lutherans throughout their history. There are many possible mitigating factors that can be argued on his behalf, but I am unconvinced that Luther should not take full responsibility for the things he wrote and taught.[1]

As we have seen, Luther inherited an anti-Jewish tradition stretching back to the time when the church became majority non-Jewish, and marginalized and anathematized its Jewish members. The Jews were responsible for the death of Christ, God was punishing them for their sin of unbelief, and the church had now taken over as the new Israel. Now the Jews were condemned to wander the earth, with no land of their own, and to await the judgment that would fall upon them at the return of Christ.

So the negative stereotypes about the Jews continued in Christian Europe, and Luther grew up knowing and believing the scandalous stories that were told about Jews. They were not only money-lenders (a trade forbidden to Christians) but also swindlers, crooks, and worse. They kidnapped Christian children to torture and murder them, using the children's blood in their Passover sacrifices. They poisoned wells, and were responsible for the Black Death and other disasters. They practiced magic and sorcery, using their secret books, the Talmud and the Kabbalah, which should either be refuted or destroyed.

Worst of all, they obstinately insisted on rejecting the truth of the gospel, and rather chose to blaspheme, insulting and smearing the Virgin Mary and Jesus himself, saying that he was a false prophet. Luther would also have heard how Jews would profane the wafers used at communion and was familiar with stories of them stealing the consecrated bread, piercing it, and using it for their Passover service. Such stories were widely circulated, and believed. In 1510 such a story was printed and distributed, and led to the arrest and sentencing to death of forty-two Jews in Brandenburg.

With such beliefs held by many in the Middle Ages, it is no wonder that Luther's own views are strongly colored by negative perceptions. He also had no contact with Jews, and met only a few in his life, who themselves had become Christians and were alienated from their people. One prominent Jew, Josel of Rosheim, asked

1. For a survey of those defending Luther, see Gritsch, *Martin Luther's Anti-Semitism*.

to meet with him to seek his help to protect the Jewish community, but Luther refused—a missed opportunity to actually meet a wise, respected Jewish community leader. Had he done so history might have been very different, as his anti-Jewish writings might have been tempered by personal acquaintance. But it was not to be, and Luther instead perpetuated and amplified anti-Jewish slander and polemic that would have disastrous consequences.

Luther's Main Writings on the Jews

So what did Luther have to say about the Jews? Luther's works stretch to more than 100 volumes, with over thirty years of writing and teaching about the Bible in commentaries and sermons, and many other books, pamphlets, and articles. Four main writings concern the Jews, although he has much to say about them throughout his other works.

Luther did not begin by writing books "against the Jews," but as a Bible teacher, preacher, and theologian he could not avoid discussing them. His early lectures on the Psalms and the book of Genesis make frequent reference to them, and his final church sermons and letters to his wife have many references to the dangers of the Jews and the damage they cause to him personally and to his flock.

For Luther, knowing what to make of Jews and Judaism was an indispensable and necessary part of his attack on the church of Rome, and his exposition of the key doctrine of justification by faith. Even more, if the truth of the New Testament, that Jesus Christ had come to set us free from what Paul called "the law of sin and death" was true, then the Jews and their claim to know how to best interpret the Old Testament law had to be put in its place.

We shall see that Luther, over the series of his writings, developed his position more and more negatively and forcefully against the Jews and Judaism. While initially he sees them as potential allies against the failings of the Church of Rome, ultimately they are a danger and a threat to the truth of the gospel, and must be refuted, put in their place, and finally, their lies and their presence must be removed. God would want no less of a true Christian, according to Luther, because God himself is punishing them for their sin and disobedience in rejecting Jesus, and Christians have the responsibility of showing them the errors of their ways and trying to bring them to repentance.

We will focus on what Schramm calls the "big four"[2]: *That Jesus Christ was Born a Jew* (1523), *Against the Sabbatarians* (1538), *On the Jews and Their Lies* (1543), and on *The Last Words of David* (1543). In addition, we shall consider Luther's final letters to his wife, as well as his final sermons, preached shortly before his death.

In the next chapter we pay special attention to *On the Ineffable Name and on the Lineage of Christ* (1543) and Luther's use of the Jew-pig (*Judensau*) sculpture. Each has a particular focus and aim, but together they give a good overview of the nature of Luther's teaching. Prepare for a shock to the system! We shall also focus on the last days of Luther's life, when he wrote another scandalous letter against the Jews.

That Jesus Christ was Born a Jew (1523)

One of the most popular writings Luther ever produced was *That Jesus Christ was Born a Jew.*[3] Here he produced his own strategy for converting the Jews to Christianity, noting how unsuccessful the Church of Rome had been in winning Jewish converts, and of successfully maintaining them in the faith.

Luther wanted to teach the Jews how to interpret the Messianic prophecies of the Old Testament correctly, and aimed to genuinely persuade them, not through compulsion or harsh treatment, but by studying the Scriptures, of the fulfillment of prophecy in the birth of Jesus. Once the "milk" of seeing Jesus as the fulfillment of Messianic prophecy has been received, the "wine" of accepting the divinity of Christ may be introduced. In this early

2. Schramm and Stjerna (eds.), *Luther, the Bible, and the Jews,* 147.
3. Pelikan (ed.), *Luther's Works,* 45:(195), 199–229.

manual there is no reference to the hardness or stubbornness of the Jews. Rather, they are seen as victims of inhuman treatment and failed church approaches by Christians who do not properly understand their own faith. In fact, Luther's criticism of the way the Roman Church had treated the Jews led him to be labeled a "Jew friend" and "Judaizer," a label from which he was quick to disassociate himself.

The treatise should not be seen as pro-Jewish, however, or that Luther is taking a position that would later be reversed, as if Luther changed his mind when the Jews did not believe. His arguments against "the Jews and their lies" are already in place, as the same Old Testament prophecies he discusses will later be used with a much more negative tone and hostile purpose. The same proof-texts will be the base for anti-Jewish verbal attacks, with the use of scorn, ridicule, hatred, obscenity, and incitement to violence against the Jewish people.

In his 1523 essay *That Jesus Christ Was Born a Jew*, Luther condemned the inhuman treatment of the Jews and urged Christians to treat them kindly. Luther's fervent desire was that Jews would hear the gospel proclaimed clearly and be moved to convert to Christianity. Thus, he argued:

> If I had been a Jew and had seen such dolts and blockheads govern and teach the Christian faith, I would sooner have become a hog than a Christian. They have dealt with the Jews as if they were dogs rather than human beings; they have done little else than deride them and seize their property. When they baptize them they show them nothing of Christian doctrine or life, but only subject them to popishness and mockery. . . . If the apostles, who also were Jews, had dealt with us Gentiles as we Gentiles deal with the Jews, there would never have been a Christian among the Gentiles . . . .[4]

The book is in two parts, each based on Old Testament prophecies. The proof-texts were popular in medieval disputations between Jews and Christians, and Luther is adding his own

---

4. Schramm and Stjerna (eds.), *Luther, the Bible, and the Jews*, 78.

comments on familiar passages. These are to prove that Jesus was born a Jew, offspring of the Virgin Mary. Luther had previously been charged with denying the virgin birth and the deity of Jesus, thereby rejecting the historic creeds of the church. He had defended himself against such charges at the Diet of Nuremberg (1522).

> A new lie about me is being circulated. I am supposed to have preached and written that Mary, the mother of God, was not a virgin either before or after the birth of Christ, but that she conceived Christ through Joseph, and had more children after that.[5]

Luther feels compelled to answer such a charge, and also to attack the Roman Catholic Church, who make it so hard for anyone to become a Christian. If someone were Jewish, and looked at the Roman Catholic Church, they would not want to become a Christian. Luther would like to persuade them of the truth of the Christian faith.

He uses the following passages to argue his case:

Genesis 3:15	The Seed of the Woman
Genesis 22:18	The Seed of Abraham
2 Samuel 7:12–14	The Seed of David
Isaiah 7:14	The Virgin Birth

The second part challenges Jewish expectations of the Messiah by discussing a further four texts:

Genesis 49:10–12	Shiloh
Daniel 9:24–27	The coming of Jesus coincides with Daniel's 490 years
Haggai. 2:9	The latter glory
Zechariah 8:23	Ten men

Luther uses Genesis 49:10, the most common proof-text of the Middle Ages, to show that the time of the Messiah's coming

5. Ibid., 77.

was precisely when Jesus came, so that the Jewish argument that the Messiah is still to come is defeated.

He goes on to argue, using biblical prophecy from Isaiah 7:14, that even the Jews must admit that the Messiah would be born of a virgin. He is sympathetic to the Jews, because Christ himself was a "genuine Jew of Abraham's seed." The Jews are blood relatives of Christ, so Christians should deal with them kindly. The apostles treated the gentiles "in a brotherly fashion" when they preached the gospel to the nations, so the Jews should be treated similarly, in the hope that they would become Christians. Christians "must be guided in our dealings with them not by papal law but by the law of Christian love." Even Christians have faults, and are no better than Jews, so that "if some of them should prove stiff-necked, what of it? After all, we ourselves are not all good Christians either."

Luther thus advocates a gentle approach:

> Therefore, I would request and advise that one deal gently with them and instruct them from Scripture; then some of them may come along. Instead of this we are trying only to drive them by force, slandering them, accusing them of having Christian blood if they don't stink, and I know not what other foolishness. So long as we thus treat them like dogs, how can we expect to work any good among them? Again, when we forbid them to labor and do business and have any human fellowship with us, thereby forcing them into usury, how is that supposed to do them any good?"[6]

Luther's closing section summarizes his arguments and his appeal to the Jews:

> If the Jews should take offense because we confess our Jesus to be a man, and yet true God, we will deal forcefully with that from Scripture in due time. But this is too harsh for a beginning. Let them first be suckled with milk, and begin by recognizing this man Jesus as the true Messiah; after that they may drink wine, and learn also that he is true God. For they have been led astray so long

6. Pelikan, *Luther's Works*, 47:200.

and so far that one must deal gently with them, as people who have been all too strongly indoctrinated to believe that God cannot be man.

Therefore, I would request and advise that one deal gently with them and instruct them from Scripture; then some of them may come along. Instead of this we are trying only to drive them by force, slandering them, accusing them of having Christian blood if they don't stink, and I know not what other foolishness. So long as we thus treat them like dogs, how can we expect to work any good among them? Again, when we forbid them to labor and do business and have any human fellowship with us, thereby forcing them into usury, how is that supposed to do them any good?[7]

Luther is trying to be kindly towards the Jews, but he still blames them for the death of Christ, argues that their 1,500 years of exile proves they deserve God's judgment and punishment, and thinks he can prove to them more effectively from Scripture than the Roman Catholic Church from its appeal to tradition, that the Jews should convert to Christianity.

Against the Sabbatarians (1538)[8]

Luther's friend, Count Wolfgang Schlick, lived in Falkenau in Saxony and was a supporter of the Reformation. He wrote to Luther about those in Moravia who advocated that all Christians should keep Saturday, the Jewish Sabbath, as a day of rest. Luther thought that this was because Jews were trying to convert Christians to Judaism—what is called "judaizing"—but it was more likely because these Christians were trying to keep the law of Moses of their own accord, especially the command to observe the Sabbath, the fourth of the Ten Commandments. Luther gets very angry with what he imagined was going on, although in fact it was very rare for Christians to convert to Judaism. Indeed, it was illegal, punishable

7. Pelikan, *Luther's Works,* 45:229.
8. Pelikan (ed.), *Luther's Works,* 47:(58), 65–98.

by law, and involved (for men) the painful operation of adult circumcision.

> Grace and peace in Christ! I received your letter and the oral request of your messenger. However, I was kept from answering as promptly as I should have liked, and as I promised to do, by many unavoidable obstacles. Please excuse me for this. You informed me that the Jews are making inroads at various places throughout the country with their venom and their doctrine, and that they have already induced some Christians to let themselves be circumcised and to believe that the Messiah or Christ has not yet appeared, that the law of the Jews must prevail forever, that it must also be adopted by all the Gentiles, etc. Then you inquired of me how these allegations are to be refuted with Holy Scripture. For the time being and until I am at greater leisure, I will convey my advice and opinion briefly in this matter.[9]

But Luther did not take time to confirm who this group was, and they became in Luther's mind "a bogey man that grew out of the Christian fear that Jews would make proselytes of Christians."[10] Luther had called such people "apes" for following Jewish practice unthinkingly.

He is afraid that the Jews will be successful in persuading Christians to keep the Sabbath, and at the time some were discussing greater tolerance towards the Jews. Luther will have none of that, and argues forcefully that Protestant regions should not permit Jews to live there. His aim is to see them expelled. Luther's main target in the letter is not the Sabbath-keeping gentiles, whoever they may be, and whether the threat of them is real or imagined, but the doctrines of Judaism and Jews, who still keep the

9. Schramm and Stjerna (eds.), *Luther, the Bible, and the Jews,* 148.

10. Kaufmann, *Luther and the Jews*, 89. Luther mentions Sabbatarian groups in a 1532 *Table Talk*, and then again in his lectures on Genesis, with a reference to the Jews and "their apes, the Sabbatarians": "In our time there arose in Moravia a foolish kind of people, the Sabbatarians, who maintain that the Sabbath must be observed after the fashion of the Jews. Perhaps they will insist on circumcision too, for a like reason." Pelikan (ed.), *Luther's Works*, 2:361; cf. 47:60.

Sabbath, thinking that it is still valid for them. For him, the Jews are no longer God's covenant people, because the old covenant, the law of Moses, has been fulfilled and replaced by the new covenant, the grace of God in the coming of the Messiah of the Jews. If the Jews are still living under the law of Moses, the new covenant has not yet arrived, Jesus is not the Messiah, and we should all become Jewish. Luther's key argument in this letter, that 1,500 years of punishment and exile show that God has finished with the Jews (unless they repent and believe in Jesus, and give up trying to keep the law of Moses) is sounded tauntingly, aggressively, and triumphantly throughout the letter. Had he been alive today, with the Jewish people back in their land, it would be interesting to know what he would have to say!

Luther was convinced that it was the Jews who were responsible for influencing Christians to keep the Sabbbath, and directs towards them the full impact of his anger. While the Sabbatarian Christians were misguided, it was the blind guides of the Jews who, like the Pharisees of the New Testament, were to blame for leading them astray and deeper into error. Such concerns were to motivate Luther consistently to attack the Jews and their beliefs, even though there was not the slightest shred of evidence that Jewish people were responsible for the Sabbatarians' teachings and practices.

Luther has two main sections in *Against the Sabbatarians*, asking first the question "how can the 1,500 year exile of the Jews [a phrase that is repeated as a taunt some twenty-six times] be accounted for, unless as proof that God has rejected and is punishing them, as they are no longer the people that God has chosen because they have been stiff-necked and disobedient for rejecting Jesus, and are forsaken by God?"[11]

Secondly, he argues that the status of the Old Testament Mosaic law has been replaced by the gospel of grace in the New Testament. He advises Christians how to argue with Jews, and rehearses arguments that will be used later in *On the Jews and Their Lies,* especially in regard to the accusation that they lie about the

11. These words are my own summary of Luther's view, not a quotation.

true meaning and translation of the Old Testament. Crucial is the fact that the Jews have been exiled from their homeland for 1,500 years:

> This is the argument: The Jews have been living away from Jerusalem, in exile, for fifteen hundred years, bereft of temple, divine service, priesthood, and kingdom. Thus their law has been lying in the ashes with Jerusalem and the entire Jewish kingdom all this time. They cannot deny this, for it is proven clearly and emphatically by their wretched situation and experiences and by the place itself, which is even today called Jerusalem and which lies desolate and devoid of Jewry before the eyes of all the world. However, they cannot observe Moses' law anywhere but in Jerusalem—this they themselves know and are forced to admit. Outside of Jerusalem they cannot have or hope to have their priesthood, kingdom, temple, sacrifices, and whatever Moses instituted for them by divine command. That is one point, and it is absolutely certain.
>
> Since it is nonsense to accuse God of not keeping his promise and of having lied for fifteen hundred years, you must ask what is wrong, for God cannot lie or deceive. They will and must reply that this is due to their sins. As soon as these are atoned for, then God will keep his promise and send the Messiah. Here again you must be persistent and ask them to name these sins. For such a terrible, long, and gruesome punishment indicates that they must have committed gruesome and terrible sins previously unheard of on earth. For God never tormented even the heathen for that long a time, but destroyed them quickly. Why, then, should God torture his own people so long and in such a way that they foresee and can foresee no end of it?[12]

Rejection of Jesus is the only sin for which they are being punished—if not, Luther will circumcise himself:

> Furthermore, at that time the Messiah had not yet been promised to David. For this reason their sinning with the

12. Pelikan (ed.), *Luther's Works*, 47:77.

calf cannot come into consideration here. Therefore let them name some other sin because of which they are suffering such misery and exile. If they should mention one or several, I ask you most kindly to inform me at once of this in writing. Then I, old fool and miserable Christian that I am, will immediately have a stone knife made and become a Jew. And I will not only circumcise that one member but also my nose and my ears. However, I am convinced that they can name none.[13]

Luther the appeals to the prophecy of the new covenant in Jeremiah chapter 31:

"I will be their God, and they shall be my people. And no longer shall each man teach his neighbor and each his brother, saying, 'Know the Lord,' for they shall all know me, from the least of them to the greatest, says the Lord; for I will forgive their iniquity, and I will remember their sin no more."

This beautiful passage embraces many points, but since the Jews always flit and flutter from one subject to another when they feel themselves trapped, you must avoid all the others at this time and tenaciously stick to the issue for which this passage is now cited—namely, because the Jews claim that the promised Messiah's advent is being delayed as a result of their sin. Quite to the contrary, God here declares that he will make a new covenant or law, unlike Moses' covenant or law, and that he will not be prevented from doing this by the fact that they have sinned. Indeed, precisely because they failed to keep the first covenant, he wants to establish another, a new covenant, which they can keep. Their sin or their breaking of the previous covenant will not deter him. He will graciously forgive their sin and remember it no more.[14]

The Messiah has come and God's promise has been kept and fulfilled. They, however, according to Luther, did not accept or believe this, but constantly gave God the lie with their own unbelief.

13. Schramm and Stjerna (eds.), *Luther, the Bible, and the Jews*, 150.
14. Ibid., 152.

Is it any wonder that God's wrath destroyed them together with Jerusalem, temple, law, kingdom, priesthood, and reduced these to ashes, that he scattered them among all the gentiles, and that he does not cease to afflict them as long as they give the lie to the divine promise and fulfillment and blaspheme them by their unbelief and disobedience? For they should have accepted the new covenant (as promised by Jeremiah) from the Messiah and received him. He was commissioned to teach them properly concerning the throne of David, the priesthood, the law of Moses, the temple, and all things. As Moses writes in Deuteronomy 18:15, "The Lord your God will raise up for you a prophet like me from among you, from your brethren—him you shall heed." For God says that he will put his words in the prophet's mouth and speak with them.

For Luther, God has been silent towards the Jews because of their sin, and their last and final exile from the promised land is permanent and eternal.

> But now in this last exile there is none of all of this. No sin is named to which they might point. There is no prophet; there is no time limit defined; there is no sign, no miracle, no manifest blessing which might let them sense God's grace. Nor is a definite place and location specified for their exile, as Egypt and the wilderness has been specified; but they are forever without established home and are cast about from place to place. Today they build their nests at one spot, tomorrow they are driven off and their nests destroyed. There is no prophet to tell them: Flee to this place or to that! No, even the place of their exile must remain uncertain to them, and they flutter wherever the wind carries them. All of this is without precedent. Egypt, the wilderness, and Babylon were definite places in which they suffered their exile. There they always had God's word and the prophets with them, and God's clear revelation. But here they are utterly forsaken, and it has been so long that David's throne has lain desolate and Moses' law neglected in the temple in Jerusalem, for which it was ordained.

Luther is not inventing new arguments, but repeating his previous attacks on the Jews. They have broken the covenant, sinning by rejecting the Messiah. That is why they have been exiled from their land, and no longer possess their temple in Jerusalem. Some Jews are more reasonable than others, who are "obdurate," but they are given to "babbling and lying." Luther's arguments and tone are becoming progressively harsher and more antagonistic.

On the Jews and Their Lies (1543)[15]

The most outspoken attack on the Jewish people, in its length and hostile tone, is *On the Jews and Their Lies*, a work of violent incitement against Jews and Judaism that was re-printed and distributed by the Nazis in their anti-Jewish propaganda campaign to prepare the way for the concentration camps and the attempted genocide of the Holocaust.

Luther's friend Count Schlick requested a refutation of a Jewish apologetic pamphlet, which was sent to Luther. Luther had already hinted he would write such a treatise, and begins by saying "I had made up my mind to write no more either about the Jews or against them." But the tract he received persuaded him to change his mind, and the 65,000-word tirade, one of the most shocking and anti-Semitic in the history of Jewish-Christian debate, is the result.

It is in four parts, dealing with "Lies against Doctrine" and "Lies against Persons." Luther attacks the Jews on three particular issues:

1. The Jews boast of being the sole people of God and they hate all other peoples.

2. The Jews willfully resist the proper interpretation of the Old Testament texts that prove Jesus is the Messiah (the longest section of the work, with many points repeated at the end).

---

15. Pelikan (ed.), *Luther's Works*, 47: (121), 137–306.

3. The Jews curse and blaspheme against Jesus, Mary, and all Christians. This subject, in which Luther becomes increasingly irate, leads to the spine-chilling proposals in his conclusion, proposals that smack of ethnic cleansing and genocide.

First, Luther describes and pours scorn upon the "false boasts" of the Jews. In the second section, he interprets significant biblical passages, showing how they prophesy and confirm the coming of Jesus as Messiah, despite the alternative interpretations offered by the rabbis. In the third part, Luther repeats the Jewish traditions he claims to have heard that blaspheme against Jesus and Mary. In the fourth, final, and most notorious part, he makes recommendations and proposals to church and state leaders on how the Jewish people are to be treated. They are to be given no safe passage in German lands, but rather thrown out of the country, their books destroyed, and their synagogues burnt. His chilling, scathing, and vitriolic tone adds to the hostility expressed, and it is no wonder his work was reprinted and circulated by the Nazi propaganda machine in its pursuit of the Final Solution, the elimination of the Jews from Germany and a systematic programme of genocide.

Luther's language throughout is violent, abusive, scatological (referring to urine or faeces in a deliberately disgusting way), and obscene. The Jews are described as "a defiled bride," "an incorrigible whore and an evil slut," they are "whoring and murderous people," "bloodthirsty bloodhounds and murderers of all Christendom." They "curse, spit on, and malign" the Christians. They "are full of the devil's faeces . . . which they wallow in like swine."

There is little difference between the Jews of the Bible times and those of Luther's day. They are "stiff-necked, disobedient, prophet-murderers, arrogant, usurers, and filled with every vice, as the whole of Scripture and their present conduct bear out." But the Jews of Luther's day are more conceited. "Their present exile must be due to a more heinous sin than idolatry, the murder of the prophets, etc.—namely, the crucifixion of the Messiah."

Luther believes the Jews practice idolatry, witchcraft, and sorcery, casting spells using the Tetragrammaton (YHWH, the Holy Name of God), which he will go on to describe in *On the Ineffable*

Name of God,[16] an additional work that accompanies *On the Jews and Their Lies*.

According to Luther, the Jews defame Christ and Mary, calling Jesus a "sorcerer and a tool of the devil," denigrating his name through Kabbalistic numerology, even calling him a "whore's son." A "malicious rabbi" has supposedly called Mary a "dung heap." They have been "accused" of poisoning wells, kidnapping and piercing children, "hacking them in pieces," and using the blood of Christian children (i.e., in ritual fashion) to "cool their wrath." Luther argues that these "accusations" may be true, despite Jewish denials:

> Whether it is true or not, I do know that they do not lack the complete, full, and ready will to do such things, either secretly or openly where possible. This you can assuredly expect from them, and you must govern yourself accordingly.[17]

Luther proposes his own programme for dealing with the Jews, with a series of recommendations for both civil and ecclesiastical authorities. The Jews' synagogues and schools should be burned to the ground, their houses should be "razed and destroyed"; their "prayer books and Talmudic writings" should be confiscated; their rabbis should be "forbidden to teach henceforth on pain of loss of life and limb"; they should be denied safe-conduct on the highways; usury should be prohibited to them and their gold, silver, and cash should be taken from them; finally, they should be subjected to harsh labor.[18]

How could anyone have written such hateful literature, expressing so powerfully, with the full armory of rhetorical devices, and with a clear logic and structure to their argument, such an impassioned call for the destruction of the life, homes, places of worship, literature, and beliefs of the Jewish people in Germany? If

16. There is no reliable English Translation, but numerous excerpts in Schramm and Stjerna, *Martin Luther, the Bible, and the Jewish People*, 177–80. The German materials are in Hermann (ed.), WA 53:(573), 579–648.

17. Pelikan (ed.), *Luther's Works*, 47:61.

18. Ibid., 61–63.

such things were written and published today, the author would be arrested on charges of stirring up religious and ethnic hatred, and incitement to violence. Luther's determined, detailed, and dark writings chill the spine of anyone reading them, especially Jews and Jewish Christians. They stir up fear, prejudice, hatred, and violence. What can be done about them? I can only call on Christians, and especially Lutherans, to not only disassociate themselves from such works written by the founder of their denomination, but to get down on their knees before God and the Jewish people, and humbly ask for forgiveness, cleansing, healing of relationships, whilst being willing to make restitution in order to restore and renew relationships of love and trust whenever and wherever possible. But after 500 years, which have included the bitter fruits of the Holocaust as a result of the anti-Semitic tradition that Luther not only contributed to but gave a massive forward thrust, is it too little too late?

Luther's most infamous work is written with venom. He liked to use "ink against the devil," but here he reserves his worst insults, his most scathing humor, his biting sarcasm, and all the obscenities he can think of, whether sexual or excremental, to lambast the Jewish people and their beliefs. The work can hardly be attributed to a sick old man, as Luther was in full possession of his powers and knew fully what he was doing. He was writing to get his enemies, the Jewish people, thrown out of Germany. He repeats all the stereotypes of Jews poisoning wells, kidnapping and murdering Christian children, and adds theological spite and venom to popular prejudice and hatred.

He relied on previous anti-Jewish writings, such as those of Salvagus Porchetus' *Victoria adversus impios Hebreos* (*Victory against the Godless Hebrews*), and *Der gantz Jüdisch glaub* (*The Entire Jewish Faith*) by one of his contemporaries, Anthonius Margaritha, a Jewish convert who had turned against his own people. From the former Luther learned about the medieval Jewish text, *Toledot Yeshu* (*The History of Jesus*), which contained extremely unflattering stories about Jesus' birth and his secret power. From the latter he learned about Jewish rituals and prayers, which according to Margaritha contained slanderous claims about Jesus, his mother, and all Christians. Margaritha is an isolated but not unique example of a convert from Judaism who turned against his people and spread lies about them, as a sign of the great pressure some Jews were under to convert to Christianity and show their loyalty to their new faith by attacking their own people at the demand of and in the service of their new masters, the church.

Armed with his new knowledge, Luther took a definitive position on a major hot-button issue of the day, whether to tolerate or expel the Jews, whom he now calls "our plague, our pestilence, and our misfortune." He states that his previous open stance toward the Jews was based on ignorance of their actual blasphemous practices:

> What shall we Christians do with this rejected and condemned people, the Jews? Since they live among us, we dare not tolerate their conduct, now that we are aware of their lying and reviling and blaspheming. If we do, we become sharers in their lies, cursing, and blasphemy.[19]

Luther is here indebted to what he had learned from the Jewish convert, Margaritha, who had written:

> This is what I say, that the more friendly, brotherly, and kindly a Christian treats a Jew, the more the Jew curses the Christian and his faith, mocks, and despises, and thinks to himself, this Christian knows that I am an enemy both to his God and to his faith, and that I curse and despise it. Therefore it must be from God that he loves me.[20]

Luther's preferred solution is that Jews should live "where there are no Christians," and he makes his position clear:

---

19. Schramm and Stjerna (eds.), *Martin Luther, the Bible, and the Jewish People*, 176.

20 Ibid., 165, quoting Margarithe in Kaufmann, "Luther and the Jews," 93 n.79, See also Walton, *Anthonius Margaritha and the Jewish Faith*, Appendix A, 104.

In my opinion the problem must be resolved thus: If we wish to wash our hands of the Jews' blasphemy and not share in their guilt, we have to part company with them. They must be driven from our country. Let them think of their fatherland; then they need no longer wail and lie before God against us that we are holding them captive, nor need we then any longer complain that they are burdening us with their blasphemy and their usury. This is the most natural and the best course of action, which will safeguard the interest of both parties.[21]

If expulsion is not acceptable, then the civil authorities in Protestant territories must be urged to practice a sharp mercy toward the Jews so as to prevent them from continuing to blaspheme. This sharp mercy is itemized in two forms, one addressed to the civil authorities, and one to the pastors and preachers (who are to encourage the authorities to do their work):

To the Civil Authorities	To Pastors and Preachers
1. Burn down synagogues	1. Burn down synagogues
2. Destroy Jewish homes	2. Confiscate prayer books, Talmudic writings, and the Bible
3. Confiscate prayer books and Talmudic writings	3. Prohibit Jewish prayer and teaching
4. Forbid rabbis to teach	4. Forbid Jews to utter the name of God publicly
5. Abolish safe conduct for Jews	
6. Prohibit usury to the Jews	
7. Enforce manual labor on the Jews	

Luther's unmistakable intention was that the religious and social substructure of Jewish life in German Protestant lands be destroyed and that Jews would be forced to leave as a result. Most obscene is Luther's rationale for the burning of synagogues:

This is to be done in honor of our Lord and of Christendom, so that God might see that we are Christians,

21. Schramm and Stjerna (eds.), *Martin Luther, the Bible, and the Jewish People*, 165.

84

and do not condone or knowingly tolerate such public lying, cursing, and blaspheming of his Son and of his Christians.[22]

Though these proposals were not implemented, Luther had some success in persuading Elector John Frederick to reinstate the edict of expulsion from Saxony in May 1543 that had been partially lifted in 1539.

The Last Words of David (August 1543)[23]

Luther placed particular importance on the last words of David recorded in 2 Samuel 23:1–7, and on his own translation of the passage, which gave a clear interpretation of its meaning in the light of Jesus being its fulfillment. For Luther, the passage clearly pointed to the divinity of Christ and the two natures of Jesus as fully human and fully divine. Jewish interpretation and translation of the passage made no such interpretative leaps, and Luther is defending his hermeneutical methods, that he always interprets Scripture, and both Old and New Testaments, in the light of Christ, the centrality of Christ, and with Christ as the fulfillment of Old Testament prophecy.

He knows full well that the Hebrew text did not bear the weight of such procedures, and wants to oppose rabbinic exegesis, which did not go beyond the plain meaning of the text (in this instance) and avoided the overtly Christological interpretation. But for Luther, anyone arguing this was refusing the light of God's Word, and must be sinful and obstinate in opposing the truth.

For Luther, the way Jews read, translate, and interpret the Old Testament is all wrong. It is confused, anti-Christian, and slanderous. Only through faith in Christ can the true meaning of the Law and the Prophets be properly understood.

> To illustrate this, I have decided to discourse on the last words of David, not according to the German translation,

22. Ibid., 166.
23. Pelikan (ed.), *Luther's Works*, 15:(xi), 265–352.

in which I followed all the others to avoid the impression that I considered myself the only smart person. No, now I am going to be stubborn and follow none but my own spirit. He who dislikes this may ignore it. It is not the first time that I wrote something displeasing to others. I thank God that I am inured to that. I, on the other hand, do not approve of everything written by others either. Let everyone see how he may build on the foundation with gold or wood, silver or hay, gems or straw. The Lord's Day will bring this to light [cf. 1 Cor 3:12–13].[24]

I repeat that it is far more meet that we believe such true and acknowledged Jews and Israelites (the first Christians) than these false and unknown Jews or Israelites, who have wrought no miracle these 1,500 years, who have interpreted no writings of the prophets, who have perverted everything, who have done nothing in the open but underhandedly and clandestinely, like children of darkness, that is, of the devil, have practiced nothing but blasphemy, cursing, murder, and lies against the true Jews and Israel, that is, against the apostles and prophets. And they continue this daily and thus prove that they are not Israel or Abraham's seed but venomous and devilish foes of the true Israel and Abraham's children and in addition despoilers, robbers, and perverters of Holy Scripture. Therefore it behooves us to recover Scripture from them as from public thieves wherever grammar warrants this and [rhymes] with the New Testament. The apostles furnish us with many precedents for this.[25]

Two Letters to Katharina Luther (1546)[26]

In Luther's final letters to his wife, Katharina, the subject of the Jews is never far from his attention, along with his health, his

24. Schramm and Stjerna (eds.), *Martin Luther, the Bible, and the Jewish People,* 191.

25. Ibid., 194.

26. Pelikan (ed.), *Luther's Works,* 50:290–92.

practical needs and concerns, and the family life they shared together. Luther thinks the Jews are causing his illness and want to harm him physically.

Luther sent two letters shortly before he died, in February 1546, from Eisleben, where he was born, back to Wittenberg. He had been summoned by the Count of Mansfeld to settle a dispute over the rights to mine the Eisleben area, which he knew well from his own family history. He would die before the dispute was settled, and it is clear he was in poor health, suffering irregular bowel movements and sexual impotence, missing home and loved ones, tired of travelling and the bad weather conditions, and ready to pour out his frustration on the Jews as if they were to blame for all his troubles. Also he wanted to emphasize the Elector of Saxony's decree (1843) to have the Jews expelled from his lands. Luther is fully aware what his influence from the pulpit could have on such anti-Jewish measures as he had previously argued for in *On the Jews and Their Lies*, but pushes the dagger in a little further nevertheless.

> After the main issues have been settled, I have to start expelling the Jews. Count Albrecht is hostile to them and has already outlawed them. But no one harms them as yet. If God grants it I shall aid Count Albrecht from the pulpit, and outlaw them too.
>
> I think that hell and the whole world must now be empty of all devils, who, perhaps for my sake, have congregated here at Eisleben, so hard has this affair run aground. There are also Jews here, about fifty in one house, as I have written to you previously. Now it is said that in Rissdorf—close to Eisleben, where I became ill during my journey—there are supposedly about four hundred Jews living and working. Count Albrecht, who owns all the area around Eisleben, has declared that the Jews who are caught on his property are outlaws. But as yet no one wants to do them any harm. The Countess of Mansfeld, the widow of Solms, is considered to be the protector of the Jews. I do not know whether this is true. Today I made my opinion known in a sufficiently blunt

way if anyone wishes to pay attention to it. Otherwise it might not do any good at all.

7 February 1546

Luther's Final Sermons[27]

Luther's final sermons end with an admonition—a solemn warning to Christians—that the Jews be expelled from Germany. He used two texts from Matthew (13:24–30; 11:25–30), which attack the Jewish leaders, and strongly argues that if Christians do not want to be contaminated by Jewish "blasphemy" they must be thrown out. Luther took ill during the second sermon, and died shortly after, on 18 February 1546. No deathbed repentance here, but a consistently hostile attitude to Jews and Judaism right up to his last breath.

> Now, the way things stand with the Jews is this: that they daily blaspheme and slander our Lord Jesus Christ. Since they do this, and we know about it, we should not tolerate it. For if I tolerate in my midst someone who slanders, blasphemes, and curses my Lord Christ, then I make myself a participant in the sins of another [1 Tim 5:22]. But if I already have enough sins of my own, then you lords should not tolerate them but drive them away. If, however, they convert, give up usury, and receive Christ, then we will gladly regard them as our brothers.

Conclusion

We can summarize Luther's lies about the Jews as follows:

1. God has finished with the Jews because of their rejection of Jesus Christ

27. Pelikan (ed.), *Luther's Works,* 58:458–59.

2. The Jews deserve to be punished, and it is a Christian's duty to remove them from their lands, destroy their places of worship and holy books, not permit them safe passage, etc.

3. The Jews are in league with the devil to poison wells, kidnap and sacrifice Christian children for their rituals, desecrate the communion wafers, infect the wells, pass on the plague.

4. The Jews mistranslate and distort the meaning of their own scriptures, the Hebrew Old Testament.

5. The Jews lie when they say that Jesus is not the Messiah.

Here is a Jewish prayer of forgiveness we might use before continuing:

> I hereby forgive anyone who has angered or provoked me or sinned against me, physically or financially or by failing to give me due respect, or in any other matter relating to me, involuntarily or willingly, inadvertently or deliberately, whether in word or deed: let no one incur punishment because of me.[28]

---

28. Sacks, *Koren Siddur*, 294–95.

CHAPTER 5

Reconciliation

What Does Reconciliation Look Like?

T HE AIM OF THIS book, *Luther and the Jews: Putting Right the Lies,* is not just to describe the historical events of the past, but to make proposals for the present and future. How can the relationship between Lutherans and Jews today be put right? What repentance, forgiveness, reconciliation, and reparations are needed, so that the next 500 years of Lutheran-Jewish interactions may become based on mutual respect, trust, and even love and appreciation? Lutherans have a long way to go. Much has already been done in recognizing and repenting of the sins of the past, both in Luther's own life and writings, and the influence his teachings have had throughout the centuries, culminating in their use by the Nazis to develop the attempted Final Solution, and the genocide of the Jews through the extermination camps of Auschwitz, Dachau, and many others. The Holocaust (Shoah) took place in a Christian country, where the majority church denominations were Roman Catholic and Protestant (both Lutheran and other Reformed churches). Lutherans bear a heavy responsibility for the things that took place, their failure to act to prevent it, and their sense of guilt remains to this day.

Reconciliation is a complex term, but is at the very heart of the gospel. In the Bible we read that "God was in Christ reconciling the world to himself" and that we are called to be ambassadors of reconciliation (2 Cor 5:18). "By this shall all men know that you are my disciples, if you have love for one another" (John 13:35). Reconciliation has profound social and political implications, as it goes beyond individual confession, repentance, and forgiveness, and affects divided cultures and societies that are caught up, often in multi-generational, violent, and intractable conflicts. The relationship between Jews and Christians has been one of long-term conflict, and Lutherans bear their own share of responsibility for this. Whilst many acknowledge this, and strongly disassociate themselves from the anti-Semitic and anti-Jewish aspects of Luther's teaching and legacy, much more still needs to be done for Jewish people to have any confidence that such teaching has been done away with, and that there are grounds for confidence that a new relationship of love, mutual trust, acceptance, and forgiveness can develop.

Recently I visited Bavaria in southern Germany. I spent three days meeting with Christian leaders, including members of the Jewish-Christian relations committee of the Evangelische Kirche in Deutschland (EKD)—the equivalent of the Church of England of Bavaria—and a Lutheran church in Bayreuth. I also managed to fit in a quick visit to the Museum and Home of Richard Wagner and enjoy some good Bavarian beer. I have always been a fan of Wagner's music, although his anti-Jewish views fueled the anti-Semitism of his age and were used by Adolph Hitler to develop his own programme for the Final Solution, the extermination of the Jews.

How do we begin to talk of reconciliation in such a tainted environment? My German friends, Christian leaders with a deep love for the Jewish people, had spent years of their lives trying to make amends and redress the terrible actions of the German churches in the past. They know the need for reconciliation with the Jewish people, but have yet to achieve true peace and harmony, and it is easy to understand why.

Confession of sins to one another and asking for forgiveness is very important, as we do not confess our sins just to God, but to the wronged person or persons. James 5:16 clearly teaches us that we must "confess our sins *to one another*," not just privately to God.

For real reconciliation to take place between Jews and Lutherans the expression of repentance and regret that must take place must result in real and genuine apology. This includes putting right the wrongs of the past, and making proper reparations and restitution in the present. This is similar to when a person is injured in a private dispute: payment of damages or compensation is made, to show that the wrongs incurred by the injured party were wrong, and should be put right if at all possible.

What Good Has Martin Luther Ever Done for the Jews?—Pros and Cons

We have looked at the life of Luther and his anti-Jewish writings, and the effect these have had on the Jewish people in his lifetime and down to the present day. So now we ask the question: what needs to happen today?

Why is this so important? I remember my first visit to a concentration camp, Dachau, just outside Munich, in the 1980s. It was a cold, bleak day, and walking around the deserted dormitories was a bitter and traumatic experience. When we came to the incinerators where the Nazis had put the bodies of those who had been gassed to death to destroy their remains I felt such physical revulsion I could not go inside and thought I was going to throw up. Such an experience scarred me, and while I had tried to prepare myself for the shock of what I was about to see, little had prepared me for the outrageous horror of what I encountered.

I knew then what terrible atrocities had been committed against my people (and many others: travellers, homosexuals, the mentally and physically disabled, dissidents, and Jehovah's Witnesses) and realized the pain, shock, and trauma that some of my relations had experienced. What could be done now to bring healing into the situation? To make a new start in relationships between Jews and Germans? To turn the hatred and murder in the past into a reconciliation and resolution of the injustices today? It's no easy task to bring healing when there has been a genocide, and the post-traumatic stress disorder has ricocheted through the decades so that even now, the memories evoke such pain and distress for Jewish people.

And like in the Monty Python film *The Life of Brian*, we might ask the same question: What has Martin Luther ever done for us?

It could be said that he came to a deeper understanding of who Jesus is, and his place in God's purposes to save humanity. Luther's love of the Scriptures, and his own studies, led him to translate the Bible into the vernacular, making it for the first time accessible to anyone who could read. For Jewish people, who already knew Hebrew, this was not a real advance, but by making the Bible available for the first time it made people familiar with the Scriptures of the Jewish people.

Luther also read the whole Bible with Christ at the center, showing how he was the fulfillment of the Old Testament promises about the coming of the Messiah. The New Testament confirmed this fulfillment and focused on the meaning of salvation, and what it meant to be a member of the Christian church. The New Testament also gave the ground for the life of the individual Christian, how to live in a Christian family and in society, and what to look for in the future in preparation for the return of Christ.

Luther's catechisms gave simple instructions to all Christians about how to live the Christian life, and what to believe. The Augsburg confession he wrote gave guidance to kings, princes, and the civil authorities. His many books, sermons, and treatises produced comprehensive and best-selling literature on being a Christian in society, and shaped the new world of the Reformation, paving the way for the Renaissance and the beginnings of the modern world.

So when Jewish people ask the question "What has Martin Luther ever done for us?" there are clearly some benefits, although they affected the Jews of the later Middle Ages only indirectly, as European Christian society developed. But the overall assessment of Luther is still a negative one for Jewish people. He taught against the Jews, that they were people who continued to reject Christ, and thus deserved to be punished, avoided, and ostracized. Luther reserves his most angry and vitriolic condemnations for them, refusing to meet with them and petitioning against them, in language so strong that throughout subsequent history his writings have been used to stir up hatred against them, and physical ill-treatment of them.

What Lies Did Luther Speak against the Jews?

Luther wrote in *On the Jews and Their Lies*:

> My essay, I hope, will furnish a Christian (who in any case has no desire to become a Jew) with enough material not only to defend himself against the blind, venomous Jews, but also to become the foe of the Jews' malice, lying, and cursing, and to understand not only that their belief is false but that they are surely possessed by all devils. May Christ, our dear Lord, convert them mercifully and preserve us steadfastly and immovably in the knowledge of him, which is eternal life. Amen.[1]

Here are the lies Luther told about the Jews:

a. The Jews were responsible for the death of Christ

b. The Jews poison Christian wells

c. The Jews kidnap Christian children, kill them, and use their blood for their Passover ritual sacrifices

d. The Jews twist and misinterpret the Scriptures to avoid believing in Jesus.

e. Jews harm Christians (a claim made in his last sermon)

f. Jewish blood has become diluted and impure

g. They daily blaspheme and slander our lord Jesus Christ

> Now, the way things stand with the Jews is this: that they daily blaspheme and slander our Lord Jesus Christ. Since they do this, and we know about it, we should not tolerate it. For if I tolerate in my midst someone who slanders, blasphemes, and curses my Lord Christ, then I make myself a participant in the sins of another [1 Tim 5:22].

---

1. Pelikan (ed.), *Luther's Works*, 47:305–6.

But if I already have enough sins of my own, then you lords should not tolerate them but drive them away. If, however, they convert, give up usury, and receive Christ, then we will gladly regard them as our brothers.[2]

h. They call the Virgin Mary a whore and Christ the son of a whore.

i. They call Christians changelings and abortions, and if they could murder us, they would gladly do so.

j. Luther's final word on the subject was his last sermon, preached just a few days before he died, summarizing the lies he taught against the Jews:

> If they could kill us all, they would gladly do so. And they often do, especially those claiming to be doctors, even if they do help on occasion, for it is the devil who lends his help and seal. They are also practitioners of the medicine used in Italy, where poison is administered to kill someone in an hour, a month, a year, even ten or twenty years. This is the art they have mastered.
>
> Therefore, do not be troubled for them, for they do nothing else among you than to blaspheme our dear Lord Christ abominably and to seek after our body, life, honour, and property. Yet we want to exercise Christian love toward them and pray for them to convert and receive the Lord, whom they should properly honor more than we do. If anyone refuses to do this, let there be no doubt that he is an incorrigible Jew who will not cease to blaspheme Christ, to suck you dry, and (if he can) to kill you.
>
> For this reason I can have neither fellowship nor patience with the stubborn blasphemers and slanderers of this dear Savior. This is the final warning I wanted to give you, as your countryman: that you should not participate in the sins of others. For I would give good and faithful advice both to the lords and to their subjects. If the Jews will be converted to us and cease their blasphemy, and whatever else they have done to us, we will gladly forgive

2. Schramm and Stjerna (eds.), *Luther, the Bible and the Jewish people,* 201.

them. But if not, then neither should we tolerate or en-
dure them among us.[3]

What Has Been the Response by Lutherans?

It is often argued that Luther was guilty of theological or religious
anti-Judaism, but was not really anti-Semitic. But this goes against
modern understandings of anti-Semitism:

> Antisemitism is a certain perception of Jews, which
> may be expressed as hatred toward Jews. Rhetorical and
> physical manifestations of antisemitism are directed
> toward Jewish or non-Jewish individuals and/or their
> property, toward Jewish community institutions and
> religious facilities.
>
> Accusing Jews as a people of being responsible for
> real or imagined wrongdoing committed by a single
> Jewish person or group, or even for acts committed by
> non-Jews.[4]

Whilst Luther's teaching has its roots in his religious objec-
tion that Jewish people do not accept Jesus as their Messiah, it is
bathed in the anti-Jewish prejudices of his time, and fuelled by his
own vitriolic hatred of the Jews when they chose not to help him in
his struggles against the Roman Catholic Church. His own refusals
to meet with them, help them, or protect them show how his views
developed from his understanding of them in Scripture to his contemporary practices of mistreating them, discriminating against
them, and perpetuating and amplifying a series of defamatory lies
and slanders against them.

In recent years many churches and denominations have recognized Luther's anti-Semitism for what it is, and have offered full-
hearted apologies to the Jewish people for such teachings. Here are
some examples:

The Lutheran World Federation issued a consultation document in 1982 saying that "we Christians must purge ourselves of

3. Pelikan (ed.), *Luther's Works*, 58:458–59.

4. Pickles, "Definition of Antisemitism."

any hatred of the Jews and any sort of teaching of contempt for Judaism."

On the occasion of the 500th anniversary on Luther's birth, representatives of the world Jewish community and world Lutheran community met in Stockholm on 11–13 July 1983 for their second official dialogue.

The Lutheran Statement declares:

> We Lutherans take our name and much of our understanding of Christianity from Martin Luther. But we cannot accept or condone the violent verbal attacks that the Reformer made against the Jews.
>
> Lutherans and Jews interpret the Hebrew Bible differently. But we believe that a Christological reading of the Scriptures does not lead to anti-Judaism, let alone anti-Semitism.
>
> We hold that an honest, historical treatment of Luther's attacks on the Jews takes away from modern anti-Semites the assumption that they may legitimately call on the authority of Luther's name to bless their anti-Semitism. We insist that Luther does not support racial anti-Semitism, nationalistic anti-Semitism and political anti-Semitism. Even the deplorable religious anti-Semitism of the sixteenth century, to which Luther's attacks made important contribution, is a horrible anachronism when translated to the conditions of the modern world. We recognize with deep regret, however, that Luther has been used to justify such anti-Semitism in the period of National Socialism and that his writings lent themselves to such abuse. Although there remain conflicting assumptions, built into the beliefs of Judaism and Christianity, they need not, and should not, lead to the animosity and the violence of Luther's treatment of the Jews. Martin Luther opened up our eyes to a deeper understanding of the Old Testament and showed us the depth of our common inheritance and the roots of our faith.
>
> Yet a frank examination also forces Lutherans and other Christians to confront the anti-Jewish attitudes of their past and present. Many of the anti-Jewish utterances

of Luther have to be explained in the light of his polemic against what he regarded as misinterpretations of the Scriptures. He attacked these interpretations, since for him everything now depended on a right understanding of the Word of God.

The sins of Luther's anti-Jewish remarks, the violence of his attacks on the Jews, must be acknowledged with deep distress. And all occasions for similar sin in the present or the future must be removed from our churches.

Lutherans of today refuse to be bound by all of Luther's utterances on the Jews. We hope we have learned from the tragedies of the recent past. We are responsible for seeing that we do not now nor in the future leave any doubt about our position on racial and religious prejudice and that we afford to all the human dignity, freedom and friendship that are the right of all the Father's children.[5]

In 1983 Missouri Synod of The Lutheran Church denounced Luther's "hostile attitude" toward the Jews.

While, on the one hand, we are deeply indebted to Luther for his rediscovery and enunciation of the Gospel, on the other hand, we deplore and disassociate ourselves from Luther's negative statements about the Jewish people, and, by the same token, we deplore the use today of such sentiments by Luther to incite anti-Christian and/ or anti-Lutheran sentiment.[6]

In 1994 the Church Council of the Evangelical Lutheran Church in America publicly rejected Luther's anti-Semitic writings, saying:

In the long history of Christianity there exists no more tragic development than the treatment accorded the Jewish people on the part of Christian believers. Very few Christian communities of faith were able to escape the contagion of anti-Judaism and its modern successor,

5. LCMS, "What Is the Missouri Synod's Response?"
6. Ibid.

anti-Semitism. Lutherans belonging to the Lutheran World Federation and the Evangelical Lutheran Church in America feel a special burden in this regard because of certain elements in the legacy of the reformer Martin Luther and the catastrophes, including the Holocaust of the twentieth century, suffered by Jews in places where the Lutheran churches were strongly represented.

The Lutheran communion of faith is linked by name and heritage to the memory of Martin Luther, teacher and reformer. Honoring his name in our own, we recall his bold stand for truth, his earthy and sublime words of wisdom, and above all his witness to God's saving Word. Luther proclaimed a gospel for people as we really are, bidding us to trust a grace sufficient to reach our deepest shames and address the most tragic truths.

In the spirit of that truth-telling, we who bear his name and heritage must with pain acknowledge also Luther's anti-Judaic diatribes and the violent recommendations of his later writings against the Jews. As did many of Luther's own companions in the sixteenth century, we reject this violent invective, and yet more do we express our deep and abiding sorrow over its tragic effects on subsequent generations.

In concert with the Lutheran World Federation, we particularly deplore the appropriation of Luther's words by modern anti-Semites for the teaching of hatred toward Judaism or toward the Jewish people in our day.

Grieving the complicity of our own tradition within this history of hatred, moreover, we express our urgent desire to live out our faith in Jesus Christ with love and respect for the Jewish people. We recognize in anti-Semitism a contradiction and an affront to the Gospel, a violation of our hope and calling, and we pledge this church to oppose the deadly working of such bigotry, both within our own circles and in the society around us. Finally, we pray for the continued blessing of the Blessed One upon the increasing cooperation and understanding between Lutheran Christians and the Jewish community. [7]

7. Evangelical Lutheran Church in America, "Christian-Jewish Relations."

A further statement to consider is the 1998 Declaration by the Lutheran Church in Bavaria, an area steeped in its Lutheran heritage, and also where the church was highly implicated in the Nazi project of the extermination of the Jewish people. They have repented much, grieved much, and still continue to feel the pain of the past and its legacy on the present. Their many statements on Jewish Christian relations today are well worth studying, and give much to reflect on. This one was timed to coincide with on the 60th anniversary of Kristallnacht in 1938, when Jewish homes, businesses, and synagogues were looted and burnt.

When it comes to Luther and his teaching, the report is very clear:

> 3. Luther and the Jews
>
> It is imperative for the Lutheran Church, which knows itself to be indebted to the work and tradition of Martin Luther, to take seriously also his anti-Jewish utterances, to acknowledge their theological function, and to reflect on their consequences. It has to distance itself from every [expression of] anti-Judaism in Lutheran theology. In this, attention must be given not only to his polemics against the Jews but also to all places where Luther simplistically set the faith of the Jews as "works-righteousness" over against the gospel.[8]

Similar statements were issued in 1995 by the Evangelical Lutheran Church in Canada and the Austrian Evangelical Church in 1998.[9]

The Lutheran Evangelical Protestant Church (LEPC) in the USA said:

> The Jewish people are God's chosen people. Believers should bless them as scripture says that God will bless those who bless Israel and curse those who curse Israel.

---

8. "Christians and Jews: A Declaration of the Lutheran Church of Bavaria" http://www.jcrelations.net/Christians+and+Jews.+A+Declaration+of+the+Lutheran+Church+of+Bavaria.2377.0.html?L=3.

9. General Conference of Evangelical Protestant Churches. "Position Statements."

The LEPC/EPC/GCEPC recant and renounce the works
and words of Martin Luther concerning the Jewish
people. Prayer is offered for the healing of the Jewish
people, their peace and their prosperity. Prayer is offered
for the peace of Jerusalem. With deep sorrow and regret
repentance is offered to the Jewish People for the harm
that Martin Luther caused and any contribution to their
harm. Forgiveness is requested of the Jewish People for
these actions. The Gospel is to the Jew first and then the
Gentile. Gentiles (believers in Christ other than Jews)
have been grafted into the vine. In Christ there is neither
Jew nor Gentile but the Lord's desire is that there be one
new man from the two for Christ broke down the wall of
separation with His own body (Ephesians 2:14–15). The
LEPC/EPC/GCEPC blesses Israel and the Jewish people.

Similar statements have been made by many Lutheran
Churches around the world, and especially in preparation for the
500th anniversary of the launching of the Protestant Reformation in 2017. For instance, in 2016 the Protestant Church in the
Netherlands (PKN) issued a declaration condemning anti-Jewish
statements made by the German church reformer Martin Luther.[10]

What Still Needs to be Done?

In their book on Luther's writings on the Jews, Brooks Schramm
and Kirsi Stjerna write:[11]

The text samples included in this volume speak their
own troubling and saddening language. They reveal the
intensity, passion, and consistency with which Luther
wrote about the Jews, in ways that are unacceptable from
our contemporary perspective. In our post-Holocaust
context, and knowing more than Luther did about just
how far human beings—including Christians—can go
down the road of Jew-hatred, we are following tracks

10. Protestantse Kerk. "Luther en de joden: dossier."

11. Schramm and Stjerna (eds.), *Martin Luther, the Bible, and the Jewish
People*, 204.

that are shameful and that require honest remembering. Because of the atrocities of the Nazi era, and because of ongoing expressions of anti-Semitism in our time as well, it is only proper to bring to continued inspection and prayerful reflection words such as Luther's, so that we better continue to tell the truth, repent, and strive for justice and protection of the dignity of life, in accordance with the worthy principles of our respective religions.

Many Lutherans have been repenting and striving for these things. But most Jewish people do not read theological declarations or books on Luther's anti-Judaism. Actions speak louder than words, and they need to see some positive actions take place as evidence and fruit of repentance. Otherwise the sense of guilt continues, and there can be no real reconciliation. One measure I am proposing, which would have a very visible and positive effect, is to remove the Wittenberg Judensau.

Remove the Jew-Pig (*Judensau*)!

It is not possible to put right all the lies Luther taught and wrote about the Jews. They are embedded in history, and rooted in the culture of his day. However, the ongoing effects and legacy of his work remain, and some of this can be changed even today. In particular, the Wittenberg Jew-Pig (*Judensau*) on the wall of the church where Luther taught and ministered remains, and it should be removed. My petition to remove it says this:

The city of Wittenberg contains a *Judensau* (Jew-Pig) from 1305, on the facade of the Stadkirche, the church where Martin Luther preached. It portrays a rabbi who looks under the sow's tail, and other Jews drinking from its teats. An inscription reads "Rabini Shem hamphoras," gibberish which presumably bastardizes *"shem ha-me-forasch"* ("The fully pronounced Name [of God]"). The sculpture is one of many still remaining in Germany.

In *Vom Schem Hamphoras* (1543), Luther comments on the Judensau sculpture at Wittenberg, echoing the antisemitism of the image and locating the Talmud in the sow's bowels:

"Here on our church in Wittenberg a sow is sculpted in stone. Young pigs and Jews lie suckling under her. Behind the sow a rabbi is bent over the sow, lifting up her right leg, holding her tail high and looking intensely under her tail and into her Talmud, as though he were reading something acute or extraordinary, which is certainly where they get their Shemhamphoras."

The sculpture continues to cause offence and defame Jewish people and their faith. It needs to be removed to another location so it is not publicly displayed on the external wall of the church, and properly housed and explained elsewhere. Otherwise Jewish people continue to experience the anti-Semitic power of such an abusive image, and their worst fears about the nature of the Christian faith are confirmed. If the church is truly repentant over such images, it must take steps to remove them from such prominent display.[12]

Not only is the sculpture an insult to Jewish people, but it offends common decency by its lewd portrayal of Jews suckling a pig and putting a hand up its rump. It also is an affront to a place of Christian worship which should be decorated with dignity and decorum, not obscenity and shocking anti-Semitic images.

The Wittenberg *Judensau* continues to offend as a powerful and vivid portrayal of hate speech and anti-Semitism. The attempt to address this by placing an explanation and commemorative plaque beneath the sculpture in 1988 by sculptor Wieland Schmiedel beneath it is insufficient. The explanation states:

"The true name of God, the maligned *Chem Ha Mphoras*, which Jews long before Christianity regarded as almost unutterably holy, this name died with six million Jews, under the sign of the Cross."

We appreciate the fact that the church decided to do something to explain and express regret, but do not believe God died in the Holocaust, and this is again an improper use of the name of God.

In 2017, the 500th anniversary of Luther's launching of the Protestant Reformation, it is time to remove this statue and replace it with something more honouring to the God of Israel, respectful of the Jewish people, and bringing dignity to a Christian place of worship instead of retaining a sculpture that is unseemly, obscene, insulting, offensive, defamatory, libellous, blasphemous, anti-Semitic and inflammatory.

Please sign the petition!

12. Harvey, "Petition to Remove the Wittneberg Judensau."

Luther's *On the Jews and Their Lies* with cover
illustration of the Jew-Pig (*Judensau*)

The petition has been signed by more than 7,000 people as of May 2017, and many hundreds have left comments in support. There is also much discussion in leading German news agencies about this, and the Wittenberg 2017 group of Protestants, Catholics, and Messianic Jews is supporting the removal of the *Judensau* as a main theme of its international meeting for reconciliation in Wittenberg in November 2017.

What would the effect be of removing this offensive sculpture? Perhaps, it would not make much difference. There have already been many apologies and much repentance over Luther's views. Many declarations have been published. But most Jewish people do not read such theological statements, and do not take much notice. Perhaps the removal of such an offensive object, and its placing in a museum, would make a difference. If something else was put there, respect might be re-established. Jewish people might realize that the Lutherans have done something to remove the offensive object. That is my hope and aim, but I know it will be difficult to achieve. An object that has been in place for 700 years is not going to be removed quickly, as it is part of German history, tradition, and culture, and on a preserved building that is part of a World Global Heritage site. Many today argue that the sculpture should stay in its position with an appropriate plaque and explanation underneath it, and that this is a better and more appropriate way to respond, creating a "culture of remembrance," where the past is not forgotten, but repented of appropriately, and continues to stand as a reminder so that the same prejudices and crimes against Jewish people should not be allowed to be emerge again, a pressing concern with the renewed appearance of anti-Semitism and ethnic tensions in contemporary Germany.[13]

Summary

There is no quick and easy answer to putting right the lies that Luther told about the Jews. They have festered over the centuries, been used to justify genocide, and are still spread today by popular prejudice and theological anti-Judaism. All that can be hoped for and attempted is that the Christian love and charity that Luther believed in in his better moments and writing will be put into practice with redoubled efforts, and that true repentance, forgiveness, reconciliation, and restoration of relationships may continue, especially in the celebration of the 500th year of Luther's ministry.

13. Bergen, *Ecclesial Repentance*, 35–56.

In the next chapter we will dream a dream of what this might look like: "WHAT IF?"

CHAPTER 6

What if . . . ?

Introduction

YOU CANNOT CHANGE HISTORY, but in the light of the tragic consequences of Luther's lies and legacy, I have found it helpful to imagine what might have been if things had not gone so badly wrong. Because I believe in the need for hope, and that one day, when Jesus returns, there will be a new creation where old wrongs are put right, and Jesus will establish his kingdom of justice, righteousness, and peace, I want to see a world in which the wars and conflicts of the past are put behind us, and a reign of peace, truth, and love is inaugurated. So I have dreamed a dream of what might have happened if Luther had not been so anti-Jewish and anti-Semitic, and looked at some key moments in his life and ministry where things might have gone very differently.

What if . . . ?

What If Luther Had Written Five Extra Theses?

The posting of the ninety-five theses on the door of the Castle Church in Wittenberg, whether a historically accurate account or, more likely, an embellished legend, marks a defining moment, not only in the life of the young Augustinian monk and university lecturer, but in the history of the Roman Catholic Church, the birth of the Protestant Reformation, and the history of Europe, as Luther unleashed political and religious forces that would fundamentally and dramatically change the course of history.

What if Luther, at the very beginning of his rapid course as the trailblazer that would challenge the very foundations of the church and re-establish the message of the gospel as the basis for faith, had chosen to affirm the ongoing love of God for his people, the Jews, and called on Christians to make a similar commitment to love and protect them, rather than allow them to be persecuted in the name of Jesus and vilified in popular culture?

What if Luther had stepped away from the prejudice he inherited from the people and the church authorities of his day, and renounced the "teaching of contempt" of his monastery's founder, Augustine, who taught that the Jews were condemned to wander the earth as "reluctant witnesses" to the truth of Christianity and their deserved punishment of exile and the loss of their land for rejecting him?

What if Luther had repented of the slanders perpetuated against Jewish people by church authorities, who used Jewish loans to finance church projects, but often failed to honor their debts, and preferred to ban them and force them to leave their territories?

If so, here are the additional theses he might have written:

> Thesis 96. That the church, and all Christians, repent of their sinful attitudes and actions towards God's still-loved people, the Jews, and recognize their shared inheritance of faith in the God of Israel.

> Thesis 97. That all Christians affirm the ongoing and uncancelled covenant between God and the Jewish people, into which, purely by the undeserved grace and favor of God revealed to us in the life, teaching, death, and resurrection of our Lord Jesus Christ, the gentiles are privileged to enter and enjoy the benefits thereof, alongside our brothers, coheirs and inheritors of the covenant.

Thesis 98. That Christians renounce and repent of the anti-Semitism of the early church that demonized the Jewish people and condemned them as Christ-killers.

Thesis 99. That Christians renounce and repent of all blood libels, charges of profaning the host, and conspiracy theories against the Jews.

Thesis 100. That Christians renounce and repent of all anti-Jewish persecutions, including the Crusades, the Inquisition, and the treatment of the *marranos*. That Christians will never allow anti-Jewish laws, or the rounding up of Jews into ghettos, concentration camps, labor camps, or death camps.

Of course, such additions would have been out of tune with the tenor of Luther's main aim, to challenge the authority of the pope and the sale of indulgences as a means of receiving forgiveness of sin. But as a Bible student and scholar, who had such a high view of the Scriptures as the only authority for God's revelation in Christ and the riches of grace, it would have made such a difference to history if he had also challenged this traditional teaching of the church.

Perhaps then he would have been open to meeting with Josel of Rosheim, listening to his concerns, and building a relationship of friendship with him.

What If Luther Had Met with Josel of Rosheim?

Rabbi Joseph (Josel) of Rosheim (c. 1480–1554)[1]

When the Elector of Saxony issued an edict that Jews were not permitted to live in his lands, do business in them, or pass through them, Luther did not raise any objections. Luther had influence with Elector John Frederick and had met him a few months previously, and the presence of a small number of Jews close by would not have met with his approval.[2]

Perhaps unaware of this, the leader of the Jewish communities in Germany, Rabbi Josel of Rosheim, addressed several letters

1. Detail from "Josselmann sur une peinture murale de l'Office du Tourisme de Rosheim." Reproduced with permission. Photo Michel Rothe Site Internet du Judaisme d'Alsace et de Lorraine.

2. Schramm and Stjerna (eds.), *Martin Luther, the Bible, and the Jewish People*, 126–28.

to Luther, asking him to intervene, which are reported in Luther's *Table Talk*, the record of his domestic conversations with family and friends.

> A letter was delivered to Dr. Martin from a certain Jew who requested and pleaded (as he had often written to the doctor before) that permission be obtained from the elector to grant him safe entrance into and passage through the elector's principality. Dr. Martin responded, "Why should these rascals, who injure people in body and property and who withdraw many Christians to their superstitions, be given permission? In Moravia they have circumcised many Christians and call them by the new name of Sabbatarians. This is what happens in those regions from which preachers of the gospel are expelled; there people are compelled to tolerate the Jews. It is said that Duke George declared with an oath that before he would tolerate the Lutherans he would lay waste all churches, baptism, and sacraments. As if we didn't preach the same service of Christ and the same sacraments! In short, the world wants to be deceived. However, I'll write this Jew not to return."[3]

Josel was the leading member of the Jewish communities in Germany, and acted as an advocate on behalf of German and Polish Jews in the reigns of Emperors Maximilian I and Charles V. He had frequently succeeded in pleading the Jewish people's cause before German authorities when they were accused of various crimes and threatened with expulsion. He had initiated private meetings, spoken in public debates, and was a tireless campaigner for the rights and protection of his fellow Jews. He even persuaded one of Luther's reformation colleagues, Wolfgang Capito of Strasbourg, to write to Luther asking him to meet with him so that the case might be put before Luther and he might intercede on the Jews' behalf before the Elector of Saxony.

Luther received the letter from Capito in April 1537, and replied quickly that he would do nothing of the sort, as the Jews had misinterpreted his work *That Jesus Christ was Born a Jew* as

3. Ibid., 128.

an excuse not to convert to Christianity. He replied with contempt and condescension to Josel about the Jews, saying that he would not tolerate them, as they were (he believed) actively proselytizing Christians to become Jews, unfounded charges he would make again in his letter *Against the Sabbatarians*.

Luther's letter to Josel (11 June 1537) is patronizing, insulting, and disingenuous. Luther says that he would have been willing to intercede on their behalf, but now cannot, as the Jews have used his previous kind words towards them in *That Jesus Christ was Born a Jew* to strengthen their resistance to becoming Christians. He accuses them of taking away any influence he might have had with secular authorities because of their attitudes. Instead, he hopes to write a further booklet to try to win them to Christ, a forewarning of what is to come in *On the Jews and Their Lies*.

He blames Josel and the Jews for refusing to worship Jesus after being exiled for 1,500 years from the land of Israel as a punishment for crucifying Jesus, and still not being willing to become Christians.

> Therefore, you shouldn't consider us Christians to be fools or [dumb] geese. Instead, you should reflect on whether God will release you from the present misery, which by now has lasted more than 1500 years. This will not happen, unless you accept with us Gentiles your cousin and Lord, the dear crucified Jesus.[4]

Luther closes his letter to Josel with a heavy sarcasm:

> Take this from me as friendly advice, as an admonition to you. Because I would happily do the best for you Jews for the sake of the crucified Jew—whom no one will take from me—unless you use my favor [as an excuse] for your obstinacy. You know exactly what I mean. Therefore, perhaps you ought to have your letters to the Elector delivered through others. God bless! Dated in Wittenberg on the Monday after St. Barnabas Day, 1537.

4. Ibid.

But what if Luther had written with different tone and content? Here is how it might have read:

My dear Josel

Word of your good offices on behalf of your people has gone before you, and I will be delighted to receive you so that we can further discuss your people's need for protection and the current edict of the Emperor of Saxony.

I have previously kept quiet about responding to this as I have wanted to hear from you and your people how you feel about this unjust and inhuman treatment you are receiving from the political masters in Germany, and try to help your situation if I can. I am ever mindful that my Messiah and Lord, Jesus Christ, was not only born a Jew, but continues, even as he is seated at the right hand of the Father, and will come again soon to judge Israel and all nations, to bear the Jewish flesh of his incarnation, now resurrected and ascended to the heavens.

I am deeply conscious of the crimes that have been committed against your people by those who call themselves followers of Christ but have failed to show his love, mercy, compassion, and forgiveness. I have been protesting against many of the injustices, abuses of the Word of God (the Scriptures), and the failure to recognize the undeserved grace of God that we receive in Christ for the forgiveness of our sins. How much more do we as followers of Christ need to repent of the sins we have committed against Jesus' own family and people, the Jews? We have blamed them for crucifying the Son of God, when all of us are responsible for his death on the cross for our sin. It was not the Jewish people alone for whom he came, but for all humanity, who need God's forgiveness of our sin. It was the church that used the crime of deicide as a justification for its persecution of your people, and this has led to great misery and suffering for them. How I wish the whole church would repent of such crimes, and beg God and your people for forgiveness!

I also long to know more of your people, to understand more fully why you find it so hard to accept, as we Christians do, the person of Jesus. Is it because we read the Old Testament scriptures so differently, and interpret the prophecies about the Messiah in different ways? Or is it rather, as I suspect, that we Christians have treated your people so badly that you have no reason or inclination to place any confidence in our words, believe our witness, or discount the works we have done against you?

I would love to converse more with you on these matters, that I might improve my understanding of the Hebrew language in which the oracles of God, our sacred Scripture, are revealed, and so that I might know personally the people from whom my Messiah, in human terms, is descended. Let us arrange to meet as soon as is convenient for you.

Your humble servant,

Martin Luther

What if a successful meeting had been arranged, mutual hospitality and welcome had developed into a friendship, and Luther, like Buxtorf and other Christian Hebraists who would come after him, had been invited to attend Jewish family events such as the circumcision of an eight-day-old baby boy, the Bar Mitzvah of a son, the Jewish wedding party and bridal canopy of Josel's daughter, and the celebration of festivities of the Jewish holidays?

I'm not sure if I can imagine Luther dancing at a Jewish wedding, or sipping four cups of wine at a Jewish Passover celebration, but, like many Christians today and throughout history, he would have had his own faith enriched by joining with Jewish people in their history, traditions, and celebrations.[5]

Certainly the history of Jews and Lutherans would have been very different, and we can imagine a different scenario, of mutual love, respect, and understanding, even when Jews and Lutherans

---

5. "Martin Luther never danced at a Jewish wedding. He never broke bread at Passover. He never shared a cup of Sabbath wine. He never studied Torah with a rabbi. He never held in his arms a newly circumcised Jewish boy. He never saw the anguish of expelled Jewish families vandalized at the hands of an irate Christian mob. He never smelled the smoke of burning Jewish martyrs. He never met Josel of Rosheim, who came to ask for his help." Schramm and Stjerna (eds.), *Martin Luther, the Bible, and the Jewish People,* 203.

agree to disagree on the key differences between them, the identity of the Messiah, the role of the law, and the place of the Jewish people in the purposes of God.

What If Luther Had Written *On the Jews and Their Truths?*

It defies the imagination and beggars belief, but what if Luther had written *On the Jews and Their Truths* instead of his 65,000-word vitriolic diatribe and polemic *On the Jews and Their Lies*? What would such a book have looked like, and what would its effects have been?

It is not for me to re-write history or re-write Luther's works, but I suggest this as a humble proposal for Lutherans as they study his works and correct his prejudices, misunderstandings, and hostility to Jews and Judaism.

First, Luther would have needed a better understanding of Jews and Judaism than that which he had received from his own Hebrew studies and his contacts with Jewish Christians who had turned against their own people in order to show their loyalty to their new-found faith and masters, the church authorities.

Then he would have needed to show the way that the coming of Jesus of Nazareth was the fulfillment of Old Testament prophecy without the vicious, sarcastic, and violent rhetoric he uses against rabbinic interpretations and the traditional Jewish view that the Messiah has not yet come because the Messianic prophecies have not yet been fulfilled. He would need to have found more gracious, sensitive ways to respond to the traditional Jewish way of interpreting the prophecies about the Messiah. He would have to develop more persuasive arguments from the teaching of Jesus and the witness of the New Testament that Christians were justified in seeing in Christ the fulfillment of Old Testament Messianic expectation.

Thirdly, he would have rewritten his proposals concerning how the Jewish people should be treated. Rather than being thrown out of Germany, their books burned, their synagogues and homes destroyed, and no safe passage being given, he would have had to argue for their protection, provision, and guarantees for their well-being. Instead of being dishonored and shamed, they should have been welcomed, respected, and recognized as representatives of Jesus, own human family, and thus treated with honor.

Fourth, he would have wrestled with the difficult question of the relationships between Christians and Jews, the church and Israel, and the place of the nations grafted in to God's ongoing covenant with Israel, now renewed and transformed to include the nations through the coming of the Messiah Jesus. For Luther, with his strong distinction between law and grace, the old covenant and the new, this would have been the hardest thing for him to change. Much of his theology is based on this distinction, which, while it has much truth, is capable of misunderstanding, misinterpretation, and misapplication, converting it into a weapon that makes Jews and Judaism the enemies of God and of Christians. Relations even today between Jews and Lutherans have yet to deal satisfactorily with this question.

Finally, Luther would have had to articulate the pattern of a new relationship between Christians and Jews, one that would avoid the mistakes of the past and show the way forward for the kingdom of God, for a time and relationship of restoration, reconciliation, healing, and right relationships. Whilst Luther taught on many social issues, from children's education, marriage relationships, town and business life, political responsibilities of citizens and rulers, his vision of a just society never included the Jewish people, and here again, he would have had to develop his thinking and provide new light and understanding. What if . . . ?

What If Luther Had Written a Deathbed Confession?

Finally, what if Luther, at the end of his life, realized his terrible mistakes, the errors he had made against the Jews and Judaism, compounded by his own splenetic temper, and a lifetime of pugnacious battles with those he opposed, and composed a final letter asking for repentance and forgiveness? Some scholars have suggested that he repented of his anti-Judaism on his deathbed, but the evidence points in the opposite direction, as we have seen. His final sermons, just a few weeks before his death, contain admonitions (warnings) against the Jews that show no let-up in his anger, prejudice, and hatred towards them. His final letter to his wife sees the Jews everywhere as his opponents trying to thwart all he is doing, and he even blames them for his ill health. His scatological humor continues to describe the Jews in obscene terms, using the language of sexual indiscretion, excrement, and rude physical descriptions. What if he had finally repented of all this?

Here is what he might have written.

My dear family, friends, and followers.[6]

> It is with a heavy heart that I choose to unburden myself to you on this, the hour of my death, with tears of bitter grief at my many sins.
>
> Throughout my life I have stood for the truth of the gospel, fought for what I believed to be right, and sought to honor my Lord and Savior Jesus Christ in all that I have taught and preached, and in the counsel I have given to princes, and people.
>
> I have not hesitated from using all the means at my disposal, including sharp invective, to oppose the works of Papists, Turks and Jews, and now realize how lacking in love and forgiveness, mercy, and justice I have been, as

6. http://beggarsallreformation.blogspot.co.uk/2007/06/luthers-deathbed-re-conversion-to-roman.html. Heiko Oberman begins his famous biography *Luther: Man between God and the Devil* by giving an account of Luther's death:

> "Reverend father, will you die steadfast in Christ and the doctrines you have preached?" "Yes," replied the clear voice for the last time. On February 18, 1546, even as he lay dying in Eisleben, far from home, Martin Luther was not to be spared a final public test, not to be granted privacy even in this last, most personal hour. His longtime confidant Justus Jonas, now pastor in Halle, having hurriedly summoned witnesses to the bedside, shook the dying man by the arm to rouse his spirit for the final exertion. Luther had always prayed for a "peaceful hour": resisting Satan—the ultimate, bitterest enemy—through that trust in the Lord over life and death which is God's gift of liberation from the tyranny of sin. It transforms agony into no more than a brief blow.

I am about to take my place before the seat of judgment of God, knowing that nothing of my attempts at good works will be sufficient to acquit me of the charges of sin and unrighteousness against me before the measuring stick of my Lord's examination, which pierces me to the heart.

How I wish I had been more gracious to God's own people, the Jews, whom he has loved and whose love continues to be upon them, from the time of Abraham down to the present.

How I long to see them dwelling in the lands over which my supporters rule, without fear of persecution, alienation, and victimization.

How I wish that the gross libels and slanders against them, which I have listened to, perpetrated, and made a hundred times worse, adding my own cutting humor, sarcasm, and venomous spite, could be removed.

How sorry I am for the injustice I have caused, the damage to their names, reputations, livelihood, security, and life itself. I realize now how wrong I have been, how cruel, how wicked and evil, and I ask my Savior's forgiveness and pardon for all my sins. Of the Jewish people, I ask for their mercy and forgiveness, that my terrible crimes will not be held against me, and that the memory of them will be blotted out from my history and legacy to the following generations.

How terrible it would be if others took up the things I have written about them and used them to further persecute God's dear people, and use them even to propose further ill treatment of them, attempting to wipe them off the face of the earth. How terrible it would be for my own people, the people of Germany, to have to live with the stain of such guilt on their nation, forever scarred as the people who so hated God's elect, his chosen people, that they were willing to follow a dictator and madman who might use my writings against the Jews as the basis for his own violence and propaganda.

Oh Lord, I realize now how wrong I have been, how much I have dishonored you and your name by going against your people Israel, and your love for them. O Lord, just as you prayed your dying words on the cross about your love for your people "Father, forgive them, they know not what they do" so I pray, I beseech you humbly, and beg for your forgiveness, that Father, you would forgive me. I did know what I was doing, how I used such negative discourse to bolster my own position and power, appeal for the hysterical support of the masses by catering to their prejudices and folk myths, played to their demand to blame someone for their troubles, and create victims to take responsibility for their harsh lives and bitter sufferings. Of course they would choose the Jews, as they have throughout the centuries, and my teachers Augustine, Chrysostom, and others encouraged them to. But Father in heaven, how sorry I am that I also turned your Christian church against your people Israel. Lord, have mercy on me, I pray, have mercy, and let not my sins be used to perpetrate further miseries upon your beloved people, Israel.

If at any of these key times in his life and ministry Luther had changed his mind, things would have been very different. The course of church history, Jewish-Christian relations, and the development of European anti-Semitism that culminated in the Holocaust, might well have changed. But we have to live with the realities, and cannot wind back the clock or change history. However, I would like to see a future based on the imagined past. I want to see Jews and Lutherans thanking God for Luther's legacy, not just regretting it. I want to see both Jews and Lutherans dancing for joy and celebration as they together thank God for Luther's life, learning, and legacy.

In my imagination, if things had been different, Jews and Lutherans might sing together as they celebrate the 500th anniversary of Luther's birth.

CHAPTER 7

Conclusion

W E HAVE LOOKED AT Luther's life and teachings, and at the history of the Jewish people. We have seen the effects of Luther's lies on the treatment of Jewish people throughout the centuries, and examined the steps that have been taken so far by some Christians to repent and put right the lies. We have asked "What if . . . ?" to explore a future of hope, of the possibility of new relationships between Lutherans and Jews, and new understandings between them.

There is still a long way to go. I don't know if it will take another 500 years for Jews and Lutherans to be fully reconciled, or if Jesus will have returned by then, but I do know that the legacy of hatred and suffering that has been bequeathed by Luther and some of his followers will take a long time to heal. We are now in the third or fourth generation after the Holocaust. If you ask Jewish people today how they feel about the terrible atrocities that were committed against their family members some eighty years ago, many still feel deeply scarred and emotionally wounded. Part of our mentality, especially in Israel, is to say "never forget, never forgive, never let these things happen again."

One of my favorite verses in scripture is 2 Corinthians 7:10, "For having sorrow in a godly way results in repentance that leads to salvation and leaves no regrets. But the sorrow of the world produces death" (New International Version). I have always understood this to mean that genuine repentance leads to forgiveness, reconciliation, restoration of relationships, and a new start. Just being remorseful about the sins of the past does not achieve this, but continues to load up guilty feelings and does not bring resolution.

I have also learned that I can only forgive others because I have been forgiven by God. Jesus taught us to pray in the Lord's Prayer "forgive us our debts (sins) as we also have forgiven our debtors" (Matt 6:12), and he set the example for us on the cross when he prayed "Father, forgive them, for they know not what they do" (Luke 23:24). So in following the example and teaching of Jesus we should readily offer forgiveness to those who sin against us.

For Jewish people to forgive Luther is particularly hard. In Jewish thought we cannot forgive things that were done to others, only things done against ourselves. Each year, around the time of the Jewish New Year (Rosh Hashanah) and Day of Atonement (Yom Kippur) there is a special emphasis on this practice. If someone has offended his neighbor, friend, family member, or colleague, it is their duty to seek out the injured party, ask forgiveness for the offence caused, and put right the wrong done by apologizing and if necessary making restitution or compensation. Only when we are in right relationships with others can we come to God repenting of our sin and asking for his forgiveness. For the ten days between Rosh Hashanah and Yom Kippur, the "ten days of awe," in Jewish tradition, we are especially being examined by God for the wrongs we have done in the past year, so it is very important to put things right with our neighbor.

As well as asking others to forgive us when we have wronged against them, we have a duty to forgive others when they sin against us. In the daily prayer book there is a special prayer of forgiveness that some Jewish people pray each night before going to bed. The prayer includes anyone who has knowingly or unknowingly behaved badly towards us:

> I hereby forgive anyone who has angered or provoked me or sinned against me, physically or financially or by failing to give me due respect, or in any other matter relating to me, involuntarily or willingly, inadvertently or

deliberately, whether in word or deed: let no one incur punishment because of me.[1]

I find it a most useful way of praying for people who we might have offended, or have offended us. It helps us to release the anger that we feel towards those who have wronged us, and the bitterness and resentment that often builds up inside. It prevents us from always feeling that we are the victims, that the guilt and wrong is always the other person's fault, and that we are the aggrieved party. Praying a prayer like this every day puts us more in the character and ways of God himself, who is patient, long-suffering, loving, and always waiting for the opportunity to forgive those who repent. His forgiveness is waiting for us even before we turn back to him, as Jesus' Parable of the Prodigal Son so well demonstrates (Luke 15:11–32).

Likewise, those who realize that they have sinned against others, in thought, word, or action, need to recognize that they must do something to put right the wrong. I travel frequently to Germany and I have often been overwhelmed by the desire some of my friends there have to recognize and acknowledge the sins of the past, and acknowledge their need before God and the Jewish people for forgiveness. Sometimes it is quite embarrassing to have people coming to you in tears begging for forgiveness and so genuinely grieving for the suffering that their family members were responsible for causing against Jewish people in the past. I think of some I know whose family members were leading Nazis, members of the SS, caught up in the concentration camps and death camps, who now are burdened with guilt and long for forgiveness. Some have devoted their lives to trying to do what they can to put right the past.

Again, the teaching of Jesus about reconciliation with those we have offended is very relevant:

> Therefore, if you are offering your gift at the altar and there remember that your brother or sister has something against you, leave your gift there in front of the

1. Sacks, *Koren Siddur*, 294.

altar. First go and be reconciled to them; then come and offer your gift. (Matt 5:23)

When I get to heaven I am sure there will be dancing. It may be ballroom with tango and waltzes, modern with disco and twist, or a combination. There'll be people doing the hokey pokey, and a large conga line. But one dance I'm looking forward to—and I've got two left feet when it comes to making the moves—is the *Hora*, an Israeli still-circle dance. It will be a *Hora* between Germans and Jews, reconciled in the love of Jesus, and clasping arms over each other's shoulders.

The Hora will start slow and speed up, with a joyful exultation at the expression of our unity in Jesus our Savior, Lord and Messiah, and a sense of triumph and victory. The tears and sadness of the past will be wiped away. The joy and celebration of life from the dead will be infectious. Everyone will be there, reconciled, forgiven, and living an eternal life free from pain and suffering.

How I long for that dancing in heaven. I dream of my family, those who lost their lives in the Holocaust, being reconciled with their tormentors and murderers, who now have the stain of guilt removed and their shame taken away. Will you come and join the dance with me? You can prepare for it right now, today. Just pray with me.

> Lord, I long to see the reconciliation of your people Israel with all nations, especially those who bear some responsibility for the terrible things that were done against the Jewish people, often in the name of Christ, and in the lands whose churches were influenced by Martin Luther's life and teaching. Take away the guilt and shame, and fill us with your grace, mercy, reconciliation, and forgiveness, so that we may live to your praise and glory today, and shine with your love, in preparation for your return. Help us to make the world a better place, help us to learn the lessons of the past, help us to put right where we can the wrongs that have been done. In Jesus' name we pray. Amen.

I'm looking for the *Hora* to break out in heaven and catch everyone up in its swirling excitement. So let's get dancing today! I want to see the *Hora* wherever the anniversary of Luther is celebrated, so that Jews, Germans, and Jewish believers in Jesus can dance together. I want to see us singing and dancing with the words *havenu shalom aleichem* ("we bring you peace") and *hineh mah tov umanaim shevet achim gam yahad* ("behold how good and how pleasant it is when brothers [and sisters] dwell together in unity").

Only then will Luther's dream of the kingdom of God on earth be established. "Not by might nor by power but by my spirit, says the LORD" (Zechariah 4:6).

Further Reading and Resources

THERE ARE MANY BOOKS and resources on Luther and the Jews. His published works take up more than 100 volumes, and there are many thousands of studies of Luther and Lutheran theology. A slightly fuller bibliography is at the back of this book.

Good introductions to Luther's life and work are the classic biography by Ronald Bainton:

Roland Bainton, *Here I stand: A Life of Martin Luther*. Rev. ed. Nashville, TN: Abingdon, 2007.

This well-written book explores Luther's life, character, and all the drama of his age. Bainton is very good at bringing Luther's spiritual and personal development into the events and challenges he faced.

This now needs some updating, and there are many new biographies of Luther to coincide with the 500th anniversary in 2017. These include:

Andrew Pettegree, *Brand Luther: How an Unheralded Monk Turned His Small Town into a Center of Publishing, Made Himself the Most Famous Man in Europe And Started the Protestant Reformation*. London: Penguin, 2015.

A good fictional documentary film of Luther's life, starring Joseph Fiennes, is available on DVD (2005):

Martin Luther: Rebel, Genius, Liberator. Directed by Eric Till. In2Film, 2003.

For general understanding of Luther's theology I recommend:

David M Whitford, *Luther: A Guide for the Perplexed*. Guides for the Perplexed. London: T. & T. Clark, 2010.

A more comprehensive work is:

Donald K. McKim, ed., *Cambridge Companion to Martin Luther*. Cambridge: Cambridge University Press, 2003.

There are many selections of Luther's general writings including:

Timothy Lull, ed., *Martin Luther's Basic Theological Writings*. 3rd ed. Minneapolis: Augsburg, 2012.

For a comprehensive selection of Luther's sayings on just about every subject see:

Ewald M. Plass, ed., *What Luther Says*. Missouri: Concordia Publishing, 2006.

For a representative sample of Luther's writings on Jews and Judaism in one volume I recommend:

Brooks Schramm and Kirsi I. Stjerna, eds., *Martin Luther, the Bible, and the Jewish People: A Reader*, Minneapolis: Fortress Press, 2012.

A new edition (in German) of *On the Jews and Their Lies*:

Martin Luther, *On the Jews and Their Lies*. Edited and annotated by Matthias Morgenstern, with a preface by Heinrich Bedford-Strohm of the Council of the EKD. Berlin: Berlin University Press, 2016.

For the effect of Luther on later anti-Semitism:

Christopher J. Probst, *Demonizing the Jews: Luther and the Protestant Church in Nazi Germany*. Bloomington, IN: Indiana University Press, 2012.

For a defence of Luther's anti-Judaism (in my view unsuccessful), see:

Eric W. Gritsch, *Martin Luther's Anti-Semitism: Against His Better Judgment.* Grand Rapids: Eerdmans, 2012.

A new book on Luther and the Jews is:

Thomas Kaufmann, *Luther's Jews: A Journey into Anti-Semitism.* Oxford: Oxford University Press, 2017.

For a good introduction to Jews and Judaism I recommend:

Paul Johnson, *History of the Jews.* London: Phoenix Press, 2004.

For Messianic Jews:

Richard Harvey, *But I'm Jewish: A Jew for Jesus Tells His Story.* San Francisco: Purple Pomegranate, 1992.

Richard Harvey, *Mapping Messianic Jewish Theology: A Constructive Approach.* Milton Keynes, UK: Paternoster, 2009.

For a collection of essays by Lutherans and Messianic Jews:

Richard Harvey, ed., *Luther and the Messianic Jews: Strange Theological Bedfellows.* Milton Keynes, UK: Paternoster, forthcoming.

Key Websites:

Petition to Remove the Wittenberg *Judensau:*

https://www.change.org/p/remove-the-wittenberg-judensau

Lament on the Wittenberg *Judensau:*

https://vimeo.com/183456942

2017 Luther anniversary:

http://www.luther2017.de/en/

The Decade of Luther and the 2017 celebrations:

http://www.wittenberg2017.us/#tab2

Lament over the Wittenberg *Judensau*

I sit on the steps by the side of the church
 And I weep
In my heart I descend to despair and to rage
 And I weep
My mouth cannot speak the unsayable words
As I ponder the depths of the pain and the shock
The horror and the rage and the anger and trauma
 And I weep

A bell sounds the hour
The children pass by
The tourists and cyclists
The men at their work
The women on their way
 And I weep

How could centuries of hatred be summed up
In such an obscene cartoon, a murderous joke
A scandalous, depraved image
Making fun of my people, my self, my soul, my Messiah

How could Israel be so profaned among the nations
That the name of God himself, *ha shem mephoras*
Be turned into the Shame meant for us
 I weep

How can those who call themselves followers of
 Messiah
Worship in this place—when on the wall is such an
 obscene insult to His people?
How can those who say "That Jesus Christ was
 born a Jew"
Make Jewish babies breastfeed from a pig?
How can Jews believe the Jews' good news
When this building shows them wallowing in
 pig's filth and excrement?
 I weep

How could I worship God in such a place that has
 been so desecrated by such filth?
How could God be present in such a place where
 His name is so dishonored?
Cleanse this place O Lord, redeem it, set it free from
 its legacy of hatred, contempt, and abuse of Your
 own character and people.
Change this place, O Lord, to be a place where Your
 gospel is truly proclaimed,
And Jewish people could feel welcomed, not despised
And Yeshua himself, the Jewish Messiah, could dwell
 in this place by Your Spirit's presence.

For godly grief produces repentance that leads to
 salvation and brings no regret
But worldly grief produces death

Lord, have mercy on Your people—on Your people
 Israel, and on Your church

Pardon us, forgive us, renew us, cleanse us, heal us, reconcile us, restore us

Lord, have mercy

Yeshua Hamashiach Adonai—Rachem Na—Alai—Choteh.
(LORD Yeshua the Messiah—have mercy on me—a sinner)

Written in tears of pain—Wittenberg 15 June 2016

Now set to music by Alexander Dietze and online
at https://vimeo.com/183456942

Richard Harvey and Cranach's *Martin Luther*

Bibliography

Agobard of Lyon. "On the Insolence of the Jews to Louis the Pious (826/827)." Translated by W. L. North from *Agobardi Lugdunensis Opera Omnia, Opusculum XI*, edited by L. Van Acker, 191–95. Corpus Christianorum. Continuatio Mediaevalis 52. Turnholt: Brepols, 1981. https://apps.carleton.edu/curricular/mars/assets/Agobard_on_the_Insolence_of_the_Jews_for_MARS_Website.pdf.

Bainton, Ronald. *Here I Stand—A Life of Martin Luther*. Rev. ed. New York: Bainton, 2007.

Bergen, Jeremy M. *Ecclesial Repentance: The Churches Confront Their Sinful Pasts*. London: T. & T. Clark, 2011.

Darby, Michael. *The Emergence of the Hebrew Christian Movement in Nineteenth-Century Britain*. Leiden: Brill, 2010.

Evangelical Lutheran Church in America. "Christian-Jewish Relations: Declaration of the Evangelical Lutheran Church in America to the Jewish Community". 1994. https://www.jewishvirtuallibrary.org/declaration-of-the-evangelical-lutheran-church-in-america-to-the-jewish-community.

Falk, Avner. *Anti-semitism: A History and Psychoanalysis of Contemporary Hatred*. Westport, CT: Greenwood, 2008.

Fredricksen, Paula. *Augustine and the Jews: A Christian Defense of Jews and Judaism*. Yale: Yale University Press, 2011.

General Conference of Evangelical Protestant Churches. "Position Statements." http://www.gcepc.us/position-statements.html.

Gritsch, Eric W. *Martin Luther's Anti-Semitism: Against His Better Judgment*. Grand Rapids: Eerdmans, 2012.

Hannam, Charles. *A Boy in Your Situation*. Oxford: Adlib, 1988.

Harvey, Richard. "14 February 1349: St Valentine's Day Massacre sees 900 Jews Burnt Alive". https://messianicjewishhistory.wordpress.com/2016/02/14/14-february-1349-st-valentines-day-massacre-sees-900-jews-burnt-alive-otdimjh/.

———. "13 September 2001. Lutherans Reflect on Antisemitism and Anti-Judaism #otdimjh." https://messianicjewishhistory.

wordpress.com/2015/09/13/13-september-2001-lutherans-reflect-on-antisemitism-and-anti-judaism-otdimjh/. Statement reproduced from http://www.sacredheart.edu/faithservice/centerfor christianandjewishunderstanding/documentsandstatements/ consultationofthelutheranworldfederationseptember132001/.

————. *But I'm Jewish: A Jew for Jesus Tells His Story.* San Francisco: Purple Pomegranate, 1992.

————. "The Conversion of Non-Jews to Messianic Judaism: A Test-Case of Membership and Identity in a New Religious Movement". Paper presented to the World Congress of Jewish Studies, Hebrew University, Jerusalem, 2013. https://www.academia.edu/5383494/Conversion_of_Non-Jews_to_ Messianic_Judaism_-_Membership_and_Identity_Issues.

————. "Lament on the Wittenberg Judensau." https://vimeo.com/183456942.

————, ed. *Luther and the Messianic Jews: Strange Theological Bedfellows,* Milton Keynes, UK: Paternoster, forthcoming.

————. *Mapping Messianic Jewish Theology: A Constructive Approach.* Milton Keynes, UK: Paternoster, 2009.

————. "Petition to Remove the Wittenberg Judensau". 2016. https://www. change.org/p/remove-the-wittenberg-judensau.

Herford, R. Travers. *Pirke Aboth, The Ethics of the Talmud: Sayings of the Fathers* Text, Complete Translation, and Commentaries. New York: Schocken, 1987.

Hermann, Rudolph, Gerhard Ebeling, et al., eds. *Martin Luthers Werke: Kritische Gesamtausgabe.* 67 vols. Weimar: Böhlau, 1883–1997. (= Weimarer Ausgabe (WA))

Hsia, Ronnie Po-chia. *Trent 1475: The Story of a Ritual Murder.* Rev. ed. Yale: Yale University Press, 1996.

International Council of Wittenberg 2017. "Wittenberg 2017." http://www. wittenberg2017.us/#tab2.

Johnson, Paul. *History of the Jews.* London: Weidenfeld & Nicolson, 1995.

Kaufmann, Thomas. "Luther and the Jews." In *Jews, Judaism, and the Reformation in Sixteenth-Century Germany,* edited by Dean Phillip Bell and Stephen G. Burnett, 69–104. SCEH 37. Leiden: Brill, 2006.

————. *Luther's Jews: A Journey into Anti-Semitism.* Oxford: Oxford University Press, 2017.

Kester, Daniel. "Hirschland Family". http://www.thekesters.net/Genealogy/ Hirschland.html.

Kittelson, James. "Luther and Modern Church History." In *The Cambridge Companion to Martin Luther,* edited by Donald K. McKim, 259–71. Cambridge: Cambridge University Press, 2003.

Langmuir, Gavin. "From Anti-Judaism to Antisemitism." http://www.faculty. umb.edu/lawrence_blum/courses/290h_09/Handout1.pdf.

Lull, Timothy, ed. *Martin Luther's Basic Theological Writings.* 3rd ed. Minneapolis: Augsburg, 2012.

Luther, Martin. "The Small Catechism". Translation by Robert E. Smith from the German text, printed in *Triglot Concordia: The Symbolical Books of the Ev. Lutheran Church*, 538–59. St. Louis: Concordia Publishing House, 1921.

The Luther Memorials Foundation of Saxony-Anhalt (Stiftung Luthergedenkstätten in Sachsen-Anhalt Governmental Office). "Luther 2017." http://www.luther2017.de/en/.

Lutheran Church of Bavaria. "A Declaration of the Lutheran Church of Bavaria: 'Christians and Jews' (June 1999)." http://www.sacredheart.edu/faithservice/ centerforchristianandjewishunderstanding/documentsandstatements/ adeclarationofthelutheranchurchofbavariachristiansandjewsjune1999/. The translation was made from the document as printed in *Freiburger Rundbrief* 6.3 (1999) 191–97.

Lutheran Church—Missouri Synod (LCMS). "What Is the Missouri Synod's Response to the Anti-Semitic Statements Made by Luther?" 1983 Statement. https://www.lcms.org/faqs/lcmsviews#antisemitic.

MacCulloch, Diarmaid. *Reformation: Europe's House Divided, 1490–1700*. London: Penguin, 2004.

McKim, Donald K., ed. *Cambridge Companion to Martin Luther*. Cambridge: Cambridge University Press, 2008.

Morgenstern, Matthias, ed. *Von den Juden und Ihren Lügen: Neu bearbeitet und kommentiert von Matthias Morgenstern mit einem Geleitwort von Heinrich Bedford-Strohm*. Ratsvorsitzender der EKD Gebundene Ausgabe. 3rd ed. Berlin: Berlin University Press, 2016.

Pelikan, Jaroslav, and Helmut T. Lehman, eds. *Luther's Works*. American Edition. 55 vols. St. Louis, MO: Concordia, 1959–2002.

Pettegree, Andrew. *Brand Luther: How an Unheralded Monk Turned His Small Town into a Center of Publishing, Made Himself the Most Famous Man in Europe—and Started the Protestant Reformation*. London: Penguin, 2015.

Pickles, Eric. "A Definition of Antisemitism." 2016. https://www.gov.uk/ government/speeches/a-definition-of-antisemitism.

Plass, Ewald M., ed. *What Luther Says*. St. Louis, MO: Concordia, 2006.

Probst, Christopher J. *Demonizing the Jews: Luther and the Protestant Church in Nazi Germany*. Bloomington, IN: Indiana University Press, 2012.

Protestantse Kerk. "Luther en de joden: dossier." https://www.protestantsekerk. nl/themas/kerk-en-israel/luther-en-de-joden/luther-en-de-joden. English translation can be found at http://www.worldjewishcongress. org/en/news/jews-welcome-dutch-church-declaration-calling-martin-luthers-anti-semitism-unacceptable-4-1-2016.

Sacks, Jonathan. *Koren Siddur*. Jerusalem: Keter, 2009.

Schneer, Jonathan. *The Balfour Declaration: The Origins of the Arab-Israeli Conflict*. London: Bloomsbury, 2011.

Schonfield, Hugh. *The History of Jewish Christianity*. London: Duckworth, 1933.

Schramm, Brooks, and Kirsi I. Stjerna, eds. *Martin Luther, the Bible, and the Jewish People: A Reader*. Minneapolis: Fortress, 2012.

Walton, Michael T. *Anthonius Margaritha and the Jewish Faith: Jewish Life and Conversion in Sixteenth-Century Germany.* Detroit: Wayne State University Press, 2012.

Whitford, David M. *Luther: A Guide for the Perplexed.* Guides for the Perplexed. London: T. & T. Clark, 2010.

Lightning Source UK Ltd.
Milton Keynes UK
UKHW010112111222
413712UK00006B/96